TACKLING SOCIAL DISADVANTAGE
THROUGH TEACHER EDUCATION

Critical Guides for
Teacher Educators

You might also like the following books in this series from Critical Publishing.

Ability Grouping in Primary Schools: Case Studies and Critical Debates
Rachel Marks
978-1-910391-24-2

Beginning Teachers' Learning: Making Experience Count
Katharine Burn, Hazel Hagger and Trevor Mutton
978-1-910391-17-4

Coteaching in Teacher Education: Innovative Pedagogy for Excellence
Colette Murphy
978-1-910391-82-2

Developing Creative and Critical Educational Practitioners
Victoria Door
978-1-909682-37-5

Developing Outstanding Practice in School-based Teacher Education
Edited by Kim Jones and Elizabeth White
978-1-909682-41-2

Evidence-based Teaching in Primary Education
Edited by Val Poultney
978-1-911106-46-3

How Do Expert Primary Classteachers Really Work?
Tony Eaude
978-1-909330-01-6

Post Compulsory Teacher Educators
Edited by Jim Crawley
978-1-910391-86-0

Teacher Status and Professional Learning: The Place Model
Linda Clarke
978-1-910391-46-4

Theories of Professional Learning
Carey Philpott
978-1-909682-33-7

Our titles are also available in a range of electronic formats. To order please go to our website www.criticalpublishing.com or contact our distributor NBN International by telephoning 01752 202301 or emailing orders@nbninternational.com.

TACKLING SOCIAL DISADVANTAGE
THROUGH TEACHER EDUCATION

Series Editor: Ian Menter

Ian Thompson

First published in 2017 by Critical Publishing Ltd

British Library Cataloguing in Publication Data
A CIP record for this book is available from the British Library

ISBN: 978-1-912096-61-9

This book is also available in the following e-book formats:
MOBI: 978-1-912096-60-2
EPUB: 978-1-912096-59-6
Adobe e-book reader: 978-1-912096-58-9

Cover and text design by Greensplash Limited
Project management by Out of House Publishing
Printed in the UK by 4edge, Essex

Critical Publishing
3 Connaught Road
St Albans
AL3 5RX
United Kingdom
www.criticalpublishing.com

Paper from responsible sources

CONTENTS

Foreword   *vi*

About the series editor and author   *vii*

Chapter 1   The policy and practice of disadvantage in education in the UK   1

Chapter 2   Tackling social disadvantage in the classroom   15

Chapter 3   Challenging misconceptions of disadvantage   28

Chapter 4   Language, literacy and disadvantage   40

Chapter 5   Researching poverty and teacher education   53

References   *64*

Index   *72*

FOREWORD

Since launching the series *Critical Guides for Teacher Education* in 2014, the need for such volumes seems to be growing enormously. When we started the series we were acutely aware that there were many parts of the world where teacher education was becoming increasingly diverse in its organisation, structure and curriculum. Furthermore, an increasing range of participants were being asked to take responsibility for supporting the introduction of new members into the profession and for ensuring their continuing learning and development. It is certainly my belief that earlier volumes in the series have helped significantly in providing the kinds of research-based insights that will support the development of high-quality teacher learning and development in whatever context it is taking place.

There has also over recent years been a groundswell of interest in the idea of evidence-based teaching (EBT) as it is often referred to. In schools all around England and indeed, the rest of the UK and beyond, we have seen teachers seeking to improve their own teaching and to improve the quality of education in their schools through gathering and analysing evidence. To some extent this has always been an element of good teaching practice but, under the influence of these developments, such approaches have become both more systematic and more public; that is, they have involved professional sharing and learning.

Indeed, in a similar vein, the widely cited report of the inquiry undertaken by the British Educational Research Association (BERA) in collaboration with the Royal Society for the Arts, Manufactures and Commerce (RSA) (BERA-RSA, 2014) has offered evidence for the importance of a systematic approach to the use of research and evidence in high-quality teacher education, including the learning of practising teachers. That report suggested that all teachers should have an entitlement to become 'research literate'.

In this volume, Ian Thompson brings a critical, research-based perspective to what is one of the most pressing issues in education: the relationship between poverty and learning. This sadly enduring issue (Wedge and Prosser, 1973) has long been the subject of political debate and also of research. What Ian does very successfully in this volume is to provide a very clear pathway through the available evidence. I have no doubt that this account will be enormously helpful to those who are engaging in teacher education – both pre- and in-service – and who share a commitment to overcoming the pernicious effects of poverty on learning and to avoid the sometimes deeply flawed explanations that are all too frequently offered by politicians and others for the continuing links between social and educational disadvantage. Where Jones (2011), Dorling (2015), Hanley (2016) and Crossley (2017) give us powerful accounts of the wider damage done by such discourses and social division, Ian goes into detail about the educational implications both of material poverty and of the ideological aspects. This is likely to become a key text for all those involved in teacher education who have a social justice orientation.

Ian Menter, Series Editor
Emeritus Professor of Teacher Education, University of Oxford

ABOUT THE SERIES EDITOR

Ian Menter is Emeritus Professor of Teacher Education and was formerly the Director of Professional Programmes in the Department of Education at the University of Oxford. He previously worked at the Universities of Glasgow, the West of Scotland, London Metropolitan, the West of England and Gloucestershire. Before that he was a primary school teacher in Bristol, England. His most recent publications include *A Literature Review on Teacher Education for the 21st Century* (Scottish Government) and *A Guide to Practitioner Research in Education* (Sage). His work has also been published in many academic journals.

ABOUT THE AUTHOR

Ian Thompson is an Associate Professor of English Education at the University of Oxford where he teaches on the PGCE and Masters in Learning and Teaching. He taught English for 16 years in comprehensive secondary schools. He researches in the areas of English and literacy teaching, teacher education, collaborative learning and social exclusion. These projects are linked through a commitment to researching social justice in education and the learning of those who face disadvantage.

CHAPTER 1 | THE POLICY AND PRACTICE OF DISADVANTAGE IN EDUCATION IN THE UK

CRITICAL **ISSUES**

- *What is the history of previous policy attempts to both define disadvantage and address the consequences of disadvantage in schools in the UK?*

- *What are some of the key differences in policy and practice across the four jurisdictions of the UK?*

- *What are the policy implications behind uses by governments of terms such as 'social justice', 'social mobility' and 'social inclusion'?*

- *What are the implications for social disadvantage of current austerity government policies and pressures of performativity on schools?*

- *What are some of the key challenges for both initial teacher education and continuous professional development in schools?*

Introduction

Education matters to all young people. In the best of circumstances, education can offer many young people hope through the possibility of change for both themselves and the world around them (eg Ayers, 1995). Yet as both the Russian educational psychologist Vygotsky (1987) and the American psychologist Bruner (1960) argued long ago, education is not neutral. School education is necessarily social but it is not necessarily just. Children from disadvantaged socio-economic backgrounds, with social, emotional or behavioural difficulties, or with disabilities, are more likely to do significantly worse at school than their relatively more affluent or fortunate peers. They are less likely to be in well-resourced and successful schools. Factors of social class, ethnicity, language, gender and socio-economic status remain the most prominent variables for all aspects of well-being such as health, education and access to public resources. This book aims to both understand the effects of disadvantage on young people and to explore some of the lessons from research on ways these can be addressed by teachers and schools.

Much education policy discourse adopted by successive governments in the UK has sought to address questions of how best to combat disadvantage, but educational inequalities persist (eg Ball, 2016; Raffo et al., 2007; Strand, 2014). This is an ethical issue and not one as a society that we can afford to ignore. Most teachers have a strong sense of social justice and care deeply about the children that they teach. Yet questions remain concerning:

> » what teachers can do to address these issues given the constraints of teaching in an education system dominated by issues of performativity (Ball, 2006);

> » what we can learn from the research literature on education and inequality;

> » and the role of teacher education at both pre-service and in-service in tackling social disadvantage.

This first chapter looks at the history of previous policy attempts to both define disadvantage and address the consequences of disadvantage in schools in the UK. The chapter provides a definition of social disadvantage in education and maps out the policy importance of the recurring educational under-achievement of children living in poverty or disadvantaged by social exclusion. The chapter also explores the rhetoric and policy implications behind uses of terms such as 'social justice', 'social mobility' and 'social inclusion'. Finally, it addresses the implications for social disadvantage of current austerity government policies and pressures of performativity on schools and sets the challenges for both initial teacher education and continuous professional development in schools.

Defining disadvantage and social justice in education

Social justice in education is a broad term that is often very loosely defined both in schools and in Initial Teacher Educator (ITE) programmes. The definition adopted in this chapter is one of equity in education in terms of: educational policy; redistribution of resources; and practices within schools. Those pupils who lack access to these resources for whatever reason are by definition disadvantaged. Researchers in many countries have focused on addressing issues of social justice in teaching and teacher education, for example, in the USA (eg Cochran-Smith, 2010; Zymunt and Clark, 2015); New Zealand (eg Grudnoff et al., 2016); Australia (eg Burnett and Lampert, 2015); and the UK (eg McIntyre and Thomson, 2015; Thompson, McNicholl and Menter, 2016).

What these studies and others have in common are the conclusions that: discourses that blame the teachers and schools are unhelpful; more needs to be done in teacher education and ITE programmes to promote the learning and well-being of disadvantaged pupils; and that views held by educators that view educational failure as inevitable need to be challenged. Zeichner (2009, p xviii) has identified three broad theoretical conceptions of justice:

1. *'distributive theories' that explore the ways that resources and material goods are distributed amongst societies;*

2. *'recognition theories' that focus on social relations within institutions and the ways that individuals understand concepts of justice within these workplaces; and*

3. *'theories that attempt to pay attention both to distributive and relational justice.'*

Following Fraser (1997) and Lister (2004), this book is written from the third perspective identified by Zeichner (2009) with a belief that tackling inequalities in education requires both a commitment to redistributive policies that allocate more resources to those in greatest need and to recognition, or respect, where individuals, groups and their cultures are treated with dignity and their views acknowledged. It is also written from an understanding that teachers and their views on social justice matter for the lives of disadvantaged young people. Despite the current policy landscape of austerity and the myth of meritocracy in education in the UK, some young people from low socio-economic backgrounds or with Special Educational Needs and Disabilities (SEND) do succeed academically and emotionally in particular circumstances and contexts. As Thompson, McNicholl and Menter (2016) have argued, teachers' attitudes to disadvantage have a significant effect on their pedagogical practice. This book, therefore, also looks at the importance of challenging stereotypical views and learns from research of schools with positive cultures of collaboration in supporting disadvantaged pupils (Ortega, Thompson and Daniels, 2017).

Social inequality in education

My own interest in social justice in education stems from both my experience of teaching English in state secondary schools in England for 16 years and my more recent role in ITE programme. My first teaching post was at a comprehensive 11–16 inner city school in south-west England situated on an estate that suffered from extreme social deprivation. The school suffered from poor attendance figures, falling rolls and low attainment levels. A failed Ofsted inspection placed the school under Special Measures. In the four years before the local city council permanently closed the school, it was consistently in the bottom two or three schools nationally in GCSE league table results. One year, only 2 per cent of pupils achieved five C grades or more at GCSE.

Whilst it could reasonably be argued that the school was not meeting the needs of its many disadvantaged young people, the reasons for this were more complex than simply describing the school as 'failing'. Most of the teachers in the school were dedicated, hardworking and talented professionals who cared deeply about social disadvantage. Others had become jaded and blamed the problems of the school on the estate, the young people and the parents. Frequent inspections led to some teachers 'teaching from a script' and focusing on examination results rather than learning. In these circumstances, the most disadvantaged and disaffected were often overlooked despite the best efforts of many staff. Permanent school exclusions rose sharply as senior management sought to both impose order and prepare for the next inspection. When their school closed, despite a sustained campaign by the local community, many young people on the estate simply stopped attending school altogether. The educational system had failed them.

This was an extreme example of the lack of social justice in education but subsequent teaching jobs in a multi-cultural inner city school and in a successful school in a small town, as well as my wider experience of schools through ITE visits, has reaffirmed that disadvantage exists across different types of state schools. Even the most affluent areas will have children living in poverty, often without access to vital support systems, and expensive SEND provision may be the first victim of cuts in school budgets. Mental health is a growing issue amongst young people, affecting around one in 10 children (eg Thorley, 2016), and is a particular issue for many refugee adolescents (Fazel, Garcia and Stein, 2016). Thorley (2016) reports that demand for access to child and adolescent mental health services (CAMHS) from schools has accelerated while cuts to National Health Service (NHS) and local authority early intervention mental health services has meant that CAMHS has struggled to meet this need. Schools are being left to deal with more cases of anxiety and depression without adequate financial and professional support.

Teacher quality and teachers' standards

At the same time as there are increasing pressures on schools and teachers in terms of dealing with social disadvantage, there is also evidence from international research and policy discourse that addressing social inequality in education requires an imperative to improve both teacher quality and the preparation of teachers (OECD, 2016). Indeed the education of teachers has been generally seen as a key policy tool to improve the quality of education (McKinsey, 2007). Although there is surprisingly no explicit reference to disadvantage in the Teachers' Standards in England, Teachers' Standard 5 does require teachers to:

>> *adapt teaching to respond to the strengths and needs of all pupils;*

>> *demonstrate an awareness of the physical, social and intellectual development of children, and know how to adapt teaching to support pupils' education at different stages of development.*

(DfE, 2013)

Other standards include the requirements to set high expectations and to promote good progress and outcomes by pupils. Understanding pupils' development and supporting their progression as learners means that teachers need to be aware of the social, cultural, economic and cultural environments of children and the communities and school in which they live and learn. Teaching requires excellent subject knowledge, an understanding of how young people learn and develop, and the pedagogical skill needed to promote effective learning.

The qualified teacher shortage crisis

While schools are increasingly under pressure to deal with the effects of poverty and SEND, their capacity to do so has been affected by a growing qualified teacher shortage crisis. The combination of higher class sizes and fewer teachers and teaching assistants has put pressure on schools to deliver SEND provision. The National Union of Teachers (NUT) reports that:

>> *in the 12 months to Nov 2015 over 50,000 (10% of the total workforce) qualified teachers left the profession;*

» *100,000 qualified teachers have never taught;*

» *schools spent £56m on advertising for staff (an increase of 62% on the previous year);*

» *there is a projected pupil increase of 1 million to 2025 (the equivalent of the need for 1,900 new schools).*

(NUT, 2017)

More recent figures have shown that the number of unqualified teachers in state schools had increased to 24,000 in 2015–16 or 5.3 per cent of the total (6.2 per cent in secondary schools) (www.gov.uk/government/statistics/school-workforce-in-england-november-2016). These figures follow the removal in 2012 of the requirement for academies and free schools to employ qualified teachers. Anecdotal evidence from my own contact with schools and English departments in particular suggests that suitably qualified teacher shortage is an acute problem, particularly in areas with high costs of housing. Official government figures show that in key secondary subjects in 2016, the percentage of teachers with no relevant post A-level qualification were:

» mathematics (22%);

» English (18.6%);

» physics (37.3%);

» chemistry (25.1%);

» biology (9.1%);

» history (24.9%);

» geography (33.8%);

» French (22%);

» German (29%);

» Spanish (47.7%).

At the same time, targets for recruiting trainee teachers have not been met in many subjects, particularly in mathematics, physics, design and technology, computing and business studies.

Child poverty and schooling

Child poverty is a cause of major concern for all schools and teachers. Evidence from both empirical research studies and statistical analyses has consistently shown that the most economically disadvantaged pupils have the poorest educational outcomes (eg Hills et al., 2010; Raffo et al., 2007; Strand, 2014) and that both policy reforms and the institution of schooling have largely failed young people from disadvantaged socio-economic backgrounds (eg Ball, 2003).

Wilkinson and Pickett (2009) have shown that economic inequality is damaging to societies with major social and economic impacts on health and well-being. Poverty, they argue, is remarkably persistent in even the wealthiest societies and this inequity gap is damaging to all living in these societies in terms of social stability, public services and long-term economic growth. Wilkinson and Pickett also point out that the UK is among the most unequal of societies in the world, which they exemplify through examining the income of the richest 20 per cent as a multiple of the income of the poorest 20 per cent. The UK's multiple difference of seven between the incomes of the richest and poorest is almost twice as large as Japan or countries in Scandinavia. Cooper and Stewart (2013), in a systematic review of the literature, found that money makes a significant difference to the material outcomes of children's lives. Arguably, recent austerity measures that have cut school budgets are likely to have exacerbated this inequality.

Dorling (2011) and others (eg Lupton, 2006) have also shown that geographical patterns of poverty and wealth are localised and are closely associated with educational achievement. London, for example, in the year 2014–15, was both the most affluent region of the UK and at the same time had the highest child poverty rates. Research has also shown that in the four jurisdictions of the UK, educational inequalities surface in the pre-school years (Sylva et al., 2004), but continue to widen in both primary (elementary) and secondary (high) school years (Connelly, Sullivan and Jerrim, 2014).

Figures from the Child Poverty Action Group (CPAG) suggest that child poverty fell dramatically between 1988–89 and 2011–12 by 800,000 children. However, the Institute of Fiscal Studies predicts that tax and benefit changes since 2010 will mean that the number of children living in poverty will rise from 2.3 million to 3.6 million by 2020 (poverty figures before housing costs). The CPAG has revealed that:

> » *3.9 million children lived in poverty (after housing costs) in the UK in 2014–15. That is 28% of children or 9 in a classroom of 30.*
>
> » *34% of children in poverty live in families with three or more children.*
>
> » *66% of children in poverty live in a family where at least one member works.*
>
> » *By GCSE there is a 28% gap between children receiving free school meals and their peers in the number achieving at least 5 A*–C grades.*
>
> » *Child poverty costs to society are estimated at £29 billion a year.*
>
> (Child Poverty Action Group, 2017; www.cpag.org.uk/
> child-poverty-facts-and-figures)

The negative effects of poverty on educational achievement has long been a policy concern for successive governments in the UK and tackling disadvantage and educational attainment remains a key part of both government policy and rhetoric. The UK Child Poverty Act of 2010, passed with cross-party support, placed a duty on the UK government, along with the devolved administrations, to establish and monitor four child poverty targets by 2020 as follows.

1. *Relative poverty*: for less than 10 per cent of children to live in relative low-income families. For this target, low income is defined as a net income below 60 per cent of the UK median.

2. *Combined low income and material deprivation*: for less than 5 per cent of children to live in material deprivation and low-income families. For this target, low income is defined as a net income below 70 per cent of the UK median.

3. *Absolute poverty*: for less than 5 per cent of children to live in absolute low-income families. For this target, absolute low income is defined as a net income below 60 per cent of an adjusted base amount of the year 2010–11.

4. *Persistent poverty*: for fewer children to live in relative poverty for periods of time of three years or more. The specific target is to be set at a later date.

The Welfare Reform and Work Act 2016 required government to report to parliament on the number of children living in workless households as well as GCSE educational outcomes. However, the 2010 Act also required the government to produce a Child Poverty Strategy within a year; this was subsequently delayed and there was no requirement for such a policy in the 2016 Welfare Reform and Work Act. In addition, the Act sought to establish a Child Poverty Commission to give expert advice to the government. The Coalition government amended the Child Poverty Act and set up a Social Mobility and Child Poverty Commission in 2012, which became the Social Mobility Commission under the Conservative government. The CPAG and other pressure groups have consequently questioned government commitment to meeting the targets.

The policy history of disadvantage and schooling in the UK

Of course, schooling in the UK has long been unequal, and Ball (2016) has demonstrated that the education systems in the UK, and in England in particular, have historically replicated the systems of social class. Ball argues that the 1944 Education Act in practice amounted to a modest restructuring of access to schooling through raising the school-leaving age and allowing some working-class pupils to enter grammar schools via the 11-plus examination. In other words the reforms in education failed to achieve the stated equity goals of The Beveridge Report that influenced the founding of the welfare state. Nevertheless, Ball argues that the 1944 Act was significant in establishing at least some commitment of the state for compulsory and universal education. Although the Act paved the way in principle for comprehensive schooling, it was not until a 1976 Labour Government Act that local educational authorities were required to move towards comprehensive education. Even then, the process was piecemeal, fragmentary and controversial (Reynolds, Sullivan and Murgatroyd, 1987).

The Conservative introduction of The Education Reform Act 1988 began the process of devolving some powers away from local authorities to schools and headteachers. It also introduced an element of choice for parents for their children's school. This of course favoured those parents with the social capital needed to navigate this system and the economic ability to move house should the need arise. At the same time, the introduction of the national curriculum, progress levels and national tests for 7-, 11- and 14-year-olds meant that central government had more political control of what was actually being taught in schools. The introduction by the John Major-led government of national league tables for schools in 1992 based on the compulsory tests increased the pressure on schools to perform as well as increasing the marketised nature of the school system.

The more recent history of the New Labour (1997–2010), Coalition (2010–15) and Conservative (2015–present) governments has seen sustained attempts to remove local authorities, teacher trade unions and other teacher associations from the process of educational policy (Ball, 2016) and the running of schools. These consecutive governments have expressed concerns over both 'social mobility' and the failure to educate the poor and most disadvantaged in society.

The policy response in England, the only UK jurisdiction where education remains the concern of the central government, has been to combine a neo-liberal policy of diversification in types of school alongside compensatory reforms aimed at disadvantaged students with a neo-conservative drive towards a more traditional curriculum and more rigorous testing (Burn and Childs, 2016). *Every Child Matters* was launched by the then Labour administration in 2003 as a response to the tragic deaths of vulnerable children. In 2008, the revised *Every Child Matters* (ECM) Green Paper identified the five outcomes that are most important to the well-being of children and young people:

1. be healthy;
2. stay safe;
3. enjoy and achieve;
4. make a positive contribution;
5. achieve economic well-being.

This government document also recognised that improving outcomes for all children meant addressing the gap between disadvantaged children and their peers. The government placed particular importance on improving outcomes for looked-after children and children with SEND. The overall aim was to reduce the number of young people not in education, employment or training (NEET). However, the Every Child Matters agenda has been increasingly marginalised by the austerity economic programmes of the subsequent Coalition and Conservative governments.

In more recent times, government discourse that has often blamed schools and teachers and exhorted schools to do more without providing the necessary resources has only increased the pressure on disadvantaged children. Prospective proposals by the current government to supposedly increase social mobility through more selective state schools, subsequently shelved post-election, would likely have exacerbated inequality (Andrews, Hutchinson and Johnes, 2016).

The academisation process, started by New Labour as a response to taking over failing schools and extended by subsequent governments to most schools, has led to an even more competitive world where multi-academy trusts have been involved in school take-overs and empire building. Although many academy converters have done so by choice with the promise of more control over finance, others have been forced to convert as a result of punitive inspections and sanctions. This process has particularly affected schools with low socio-economic status populations. In general, secondary schools with low *prior* attainment tend to get worse Ofsted gradings. The new measure of Progress 8, which is intended to be fairer to schools in challenging circumstances in terms of context, may not solve the problem, particularly for schools in mainly white working-class areas where boys in particular have often achieved poor academic results (Strand, 2014). It could be argued that 'value-added' measures fail to take into account the debilitating effects of poor employment prospects, the stigmatisation of working-class communities and covert selection.

Researchers have also pointed out the need to replace sanctions with redistributive policies where extra money is spent on schools serving disadvantaged communities (eg Beckett, 2016; Smyth and Wrigley, 2013). Exhorting schools to do more without providing the necessary resources only increases the pressure on schools, teachers and disadvantaged children. There is a policy need to reduce competition between schools and increase cooperation in order to broaden and enrich curricula including high-quality apprenticeship schemes and vocational education (eg Pring, 2013).

What is clear is that there is a contradiction between the political consensus that education should enable all students to access the knowledge to enable them to function and thrive in society, and anxieties around public finances and the declining state of the economy. This has resulted in a series of educational policies and reforms that might be seen to exacerbate the problems of child poverty rather than address them.

Social justice, social mobility and social inclusion

The pronounced neo-liberal stance taken by the current Conservative government often blames the so-called undeserving poor, increasingly presented as 'non-productive groups', for causing the need for welfare provision. Locating the problem of poverty as an issue of 'social mobility', as is the case in central UK government discourse and education policy in England, is very different to addressing the root causes of economic and social disadvantage. For example in his foreword to the 2010 White Paper, *The Importance of Teaching*, the then Secretary of State for Education in England Michael Gove wrote:

Our schools should be engines of social mobility, helping children to overcome the accidents of birth and background to achieve much more than they may ever have imagined. But, at the moment, our schools system does not close gaps, it widens them.

Children from poorer homes start behind their wealthier contemporaries when they arrive at school and during their educational journey they fall further and further back. The achievement gap between rich and poor widens at the beginning of primary school, gets worse by GCSE and is a yawning gulf by the time (far too few) sit A levels and apply to university.

This injustice has inspired a grim fatalism in some, who believe that deprivation must be destiny. But for this Government the scale of this tragedy demands action. Urgent, focused, radical action.

(DfE, 2010, pp 6–7).

Of course much of what Gove argued here is true in terms of inequality in the education system. However, by arguing that this is an issue of social mobility Gove wrongly conflates social justice and social inclusion with the idea of meritocracy in education. The real barriers for those in poverty or with SEND are often more prohibiting and material than this argument allows. Yet, at the same time, Gove's educational policies placed the entire responsibility for inequalities on the school system rather than addressing the root economic causes of deprivation.

Policy differences in the four jurisdictions of the UK

The report of the BERA Commission on Poverty and Policy Advocacy (Ivinson et al., 2017) highlighted that though there are regional differences across the four nations of the UK, and indeed large discrepancies within the countries themselves, persistent high levels of child poverty, which have risen in all jurisdictions since 2013, remains a major social issue in schools across the jurisdictions.

The BERA Commission found some particular historical and cultural features of the four educational systems. The structuring of school systems across the jurisdictions range from: an almost exclusive provision of public education in Wales and, to a slightly lesser extent, in Scotland; to a highly segregated system (Catholic, Protestant, maintained, controlled) in Northern Ireland; and a determined commitment to the privatisation agenda in England. These structures therefore reflect historical and cultural policy concerns about what matters to policy makers within particular jurisdictions. These differences also suggest a different relationship between policy makers and evidence from educational research. For example, researchers in jurisdictions other than England were far more likely to be able to have direct contact with policy makers in education. England is the only jurisdiction where education is governed directly by the UK parliament, which also governs welfare and other policies. This has created an even stronger pressure to develop educational policy which shifts blame onto schools and away from government. Moreover, neo-liberal and neo-conservative school reforms have proceeded fastest and furthest in England.

Across the four jurisdictions, England is the only place where the national UK government has direct control over education alongside other services such as welfare. As described above, tackling child poverty has been viewed as a cross-departmental issue that requires communication between government departments. In the three jurisdictions of Scotland, Wales and Northern Ireland, the Westminster government treasury retains control of the tax-raising powers, which in practice greatly restricts how money is able to be attributed to services. Education comes under the control of the devolved governments of Scotland and Wales and the devolved Executive Assembly in Northern Ireland. Spending for all services, including education, is limited by the control held by Westminster including tax-raising powers. This means that jurisdictions in practice have had limited scope to soften the effects of government austerity measures. Nevertheless, each jurisdiction apart from England has powers over how money is allocated for education and in Scotland, Wales and Northern Ireland (and not in England) local authorities retain control of the education budget and oversee its use.

The introduction of the Pupil Premium Grant in England in 2011 (funding specifically related to the number of pupils from disadvantaged backgrounds in each school), and the monitoring of the effects of schools' spending of these funds through the requirement for schools to publish annual plans and evaluations of their use of this money, has highlighted the need for schools in England to do more to help disadvantaged students. So while national politics and the specific values placed on education within Scotland, Wales and Northern Ireland have developed independently of those in England, it could also be argued that the lack of a mediating space between government agencies and education in England has heightened the conditions for the accelerated pace of marketisation and the neo-liberal agenda (Ball, 2006). In each other jurisdiction, education policy is mediated to some extent through a devolved government or executive assembly.

Policy in England

It could be argued that many major policy initiatives reflect a neo-liberal mindset, which includes a commitment to performativity, increased marketisation of schools and sanctions to force academisation. In England, the policy solution has been partly to devolve the resources, decisions and accountability to individual schools through the pupil premium grant (Burn et al., 2016). However, it is as yet unclear how effectively the pupil premium is being used by schools (Carpenter et al., 2013), or how success will be measured given the current Conservative government's abandonment of the 'contextual added value' attainment measures introduced by the previous Labour administration. 'Contextual added value' was a statistical comparison of a child's performance with children with similar prior performance and circumstances. The lack of take up of free school meals (FSMs) in many cases means that many young people living in poverty are not identified for pupil premium support. Further changes in funding that have penalised urban schools in favour of schools in more affluent areas are likely to worsen the problem.

It is also in England where government rhetoric most often falls back on deficit models which blame both those living in poverty and the teachers who teach them rather than providing adequate resources, particularly in early education. Sylva et al. (2004) found that high-quality pre-school provision, while not eliminating differences in social backgrounds, can help to reduce disadvantaged children's experience. They also found that disadvantaged children do better in pre-school settings with a mixture of children from different social backgrounds rather than in settings catering mostly for children from disadvantaged families. Well-qualified staff with good pedagogical skills also made a difference. Yet pre-school provision in England remains uneven, staff are often poorly paid and more organised and effective child care is far more likely to be used by families with higher incomes. In secondary and post-secondary education, the uncertain state of vocational education and apprenticeships contributes to the demoralisation of many young people.

Policy in Northern Ireland

The Northern Ireland (NI) education system remains segregated, reflecting the political factionalism that has dominated the region. Government statistics show that 93 per cent of children in primary (age 4–11) and post-primary (age 11–18) schools attend largely either Catholic schools (Maintained) or schools that in the majority are attended by Protestant children (Controlled). Less than 7 per cent of NI children are proactively educated together at integrated schools. Those who achieve least well academically are boys from socially disadvantaged backgrounds, and in particular from poor Protestant families, despite the country as a whole achieving results that are the highest across the jurisdictions (Burns, Leitch and Hughes, 2015).

The NI Executive's 2016 Child Poverty Strategy 'Delivering Social Change' has the goal of eradicating child poverty. The framework for this child poverty strategy places particular emphasis on breaking inter-generational cycles of poverty through child-based interventions aimed at improving educational attainment (McCormick, 2013). NI policy developments are linked by the understanding that for children to get the most from their education there needs to be co-ordinated cross-government working that targets disadvantaged communities. One such initiative is the Full Service Extended Schools in NI areas of highest deprivation. This has achieved significant improvements in achievement, attendance and numbers of pupils returning to sixth-form study. However, not all schools serving these disadvantaged communities receive this extra economic support.

Policy in Scotland

In contrast to policy developments in England, in Scotland the policy response to child poverty in Scotland has been to place a legal duty on local authorities to monitor and take steps to reduce inequalities of outcome linked to social disadvantage. In fact Scotland has a long history of self-determination in a number of policy areas, including education, and the Scottish Office, local government, teaching unions and universities have been keen key influences in educational policy both before and after the setting up of the Scottish Parliament. Robertson (2014) has argued that Scotland has to some degree held on to social democratic policy objectives in developing its education system. This has led the government agency Education Scotland to work with a number of local authorities and university researchers to broker and facilitate partnerships within and across schools and local authorities. The solution-focused approach is underpinned by systematic enquiry and the use of evidence to address Scotland's attainment issues with a focus on tackling educational inequality.

Policy in Wales

Wales has a history of both endemic poverty (Egan, 2017) and a commitment to tackling this through education policy. It is the only UK administration to have a designated Minister for Communities and Tackling Poverty and each of the 52 Communities First Areas have an Education Officer. Egan (2017) has argued that there has been a strong pull since devolution to develop educational policies that are distinct to those of the Westminster government. For example, the Foundation Phase was developed with a new child-centred approach that was based on strong research and was well resourced by the Synod. Some policies aim to mitigate the worst effects of the UK central government policies that affect poor families and children such as bedroom tax support and support with higher education fees. Other initiatives in Wales include also pioneering approaches to support poor families such as: Flying Start (free nursery provision for 0–3-year-olds); Foundation Phase curriculum (3–7 years); Families First (voluntary opt-in support); Reach the Heights (arts projects aimed at reducing young people in NEET 2007–13); the Reading Agency in Denbighshire; and the Pupil Deprivation Grant (PDG).

Key challenges for both initial teacher education and continuous professional development in schools

As we have seen, recent government discourse from the central UK government, as well as from the regionally devolved governments in Scotland, Wales and Northern Ireland, has voiced significant concerns about levels of educational inequality. This focus has had some effect on policy and practice in both ITE and in funding for supporting disadvantaged students. In addition, devolved powers have to some degree enabled a different approach to educational policy and there are lessons to be learned from interventions outside of England. However, the vast majority of teachers and pupils in the UK are in England and key challenges remain in terms of tackling disadvantage across the UK. Given the policy climate described in this chapter, the key challenges for ITE and continuing professional development (CPD) in schools are to find ways to:

» challenge deficit ideologies;

» promote equity with limited or diminishing resources;

» develop radical curricula and pedagogies that promote the learning and well-being of disadvantaged pupils.

IN A **NUTSHELL**

The UK educational system is unjust. Although government policy has consistently identified the pernicious effects of disadvantage in the UK, the educational system remains unequal. The conflation of the term 'social mobility' by some politicians with concepts of 'social justice' and 'social inclusion' is both confusing and misleading. In effect, this allows politicians to blame schools, teachers and even the disadvantaged themselves.

Current austerity government policies and pressures of performativity on schools are likely to exacerbate social disadvantage. Although disadvantage exists across the UK, there are some key differences in policy and practice across the four jurisdictions of the UK. England represents the most extreme and complicated jurisdiction where both neo-liberal policies of competition and privatisation and neo-conservative policies of restricted curricula dominate. There are lessons to be learned from educational policies in the devolved nations.

The key challenges for both ITE and CPD in school include: challenging deficit ideologies; promoting equity with limited resources; producing curricula and pedagogies that promote the learning and well-being of disadvantaged pupils.

REFLECTIONS ON **CRITICAL ISSUES**

- *The educational system in the UK remains unequal. Although disadvantage is acknowledged, the effects of redistributive policies have been limited.*

- *The conflation of the term 'social mobility' with 'social justice' and 'social inclusion' is both confusing and misleading.*

- *Current austerity government policies and pressures of performativity on schools are likely to exacerbate social disadvantage.*

- *Although disadvantage exists across the UK, there are some key differences in policy and practice across the four jurisdictions of the UK.*

- *The key challenges for both ITE and CPD in school include: challenging deficit ideologies; promoting equity with limited resources; producing curricula and pedagogies that promote the learning and well-being of disadvantaged pupils.*

CHAPTER 2 | TACKLING SOCIAL DISADVANTAGE IN THE CLASSROOM

CRITICAL **ISSUES**

- *What are some of the cognitive and affective consequences for children of social disadvantage?*

- *What are the some of the psychological, environmental and sociological factors associated with poverty for children?*

- *What is the research evidence on the barriers to learning caused by social disadvantage?*

- *What can a teacher do in the classroom to address the cognitive and affective consequences of poverty and social disadvantage on children and their learning?*

- *In what ways can teacher collaboration support vulnerable learners?*

- *What are some of the benefits of arts-based interventions for vulnerable learners?*

Introduction

Poverty and other forms of social disadvantage have deeply harmful consequences for the cognitive, emotional and social development of children. In order to address the question of how to tackle social disadvantage in the classroom, teachers and teacher educators need to consider the cognitive, affective and social processes involved in learning. This chapter addresses some of the cognitive and affective consequences of poverty and social disadvantage on children and their learning and explores the pedagogic implications of research evidence. The chapter draws on findings from research in the educational fields of psychology and sociology to explain the barriers to learning caused by social disadvantage including pupils' well-being, mental health and special educational needs. It identifies some best practice in designing classroom and school cultures and environments that help disadvantaged students to thrive emotionally and academically in the classroom. Finally, it explores evidence from a recent research project on the extent to which teacher collaboration can help a school to support disadvantaged pupils and vulnerable learners.

The cognitive effects of social and economic disadvantage

The negative effects of social and economic disadvantage on cognition begin early in life and continue to grow through the school years. The Child Poverty Action Group (CPAG) suggests that children from poorer backgrounds fall behind their peers at all stages of education.

» *By the age of three, poorer children are estimated to be, on average, nine months behind children from more wealthy backgrounds.*

» *According to Department for Education statistics, by the end of primary school, pupils receiving free school meals are estimated to be almost three terms behind their more affluent peers.*

» *By 14, this gap grows to over five terms.*

» *By 16, children receiving free school meals achieve on average 1.7 grades lower at GCSE.*

(Child Poverty Action Group, 2017

www.cpag.org.uk/content/impact-poverty)

In a methodologically robust study of data from the four sweeps of the UK Millennium Cohort Study (MCS) of children born at the turn of the century, Dickerson and Popli (2012) documented the impact that poverty, and in particular persistent poverty, had on these children's cognitive development in their early years. They found that children born into poverty had significantly lower test scores at ages three, five and seven, and that continually living in poverty in their early years had a cumulative negative impact on their cognitive development. Children who live persistently in poverty throughout their early years had cognitive development test scores at age seven more than ten percentile ranks lower than children who had never experienced poverty. These results stood even after controlling for a wide range of background characteristics and parental factors.

The cognitive deficits associated with poverty include: a low attention span; an impaired ability to self-regulate; slow processing speed; language problems; poor memory; and a lack of social skills. Studies have also shown that children from poorer backgrounds in the UK are more likely to develop attention deficit hyperactivity disorder (ADHD) (Russell, Ford and Russell, 2015). ADHD is strongly associated with other disorders such as autism, behavioural difficulties and some mental health problems such as depression.

Psychological effects of poverty

Poverty also has profound psychological effects, in part because public perceptions of people and families living in poverty are often extremely negative. Fell and Hewstone (2015) found that social contact with people living in poverty can help to combat these views and improve both attitudes and relations. They also found that:

» *negative perceptions affect how people see themselves. Those experiencing poverty show significantly lower levels of confidence in their own ability to succeed. This has negative physical and psychological health consequences, along with reduced educational and professional attainment;*

» *poverty increases the risk of mental illnesses, including schizophrenia, depression, anxiety and substance addiction. Poverty can act as both a causal factor (eg stress resulting from poverty triggering depression) and a consequence of mental illness (eg schizophrenic symptoms leading to decreased socio-economic status and prospects);*

» *poverty during early childhood is associated with genetic adaptation, producing a short-term strategy to cope with the stressful developmental environment. This comes at the expense of long-term health, with increased susceptibility to cardiac disease and certain cancers;*

» *children raised in environments of low socio-economic status show consistent reductions in cognitive performance across many areas, particularly language function and cognitive control (attention, planning, decision-making);*

» *resource scarcity induces a 'scarcity mindset', characterised by increased focus on immediate goals at the expense of peripheral tasks and long-term planning. This may contribute to perpetuating the cycle of poverty.*

(Fell and Hewstone, 2015, p 1)

Problems in attention, planning and decision-making can have significant effects for children in both the school setting and when tackling tasks set by teachers for homework. Lack of reliance is often cited as one of the main factors why children from disadvantaged backgrounds do not succeed, when in fact these young people can show remarkable resilience in dealing with their daily lives.

Environmental aspects of poverty

Research has shown that children from poor environments may face widespread and multiple environmental inequalities that can have cumulative effects on their development (eg Evans, 2004). These inequalities can include:

» unstable and chaotic households;

» less social support and resources;

» lack of household space;

» poor air quality and pollution leading to increased incidents of asthma;

» more dangerous neighbourhoods;

» less successful academically and/or less socially mixed schools;

» lower quality nutrition;

» poorer quality school buildings.

Some figures in government and in social policy have recently argued that improving parenting skills is one of the keys to alleviating inequality. However, research has also shown that parents' social class, qualifications and well-being have bigger effects on their children's development than their parenting skills (Sullivan, Ketende and Joshi, 2013). Indeed, it is important to point out that families in poverty try their best for their children and adults will often go without food or new clothing in order to support their offspring (Ridge, 2009).

The sociology of poverty

As seen in Chapter 1, there is a disparity between some government rhetoric on dealing with issues of social justice and the reality of educational policies that further disadvantage vulnerable learners. International evidence shows that some countries are more effective in introducing policies that help to offset some key aspects of social disadvantage without holding back other pupils. For example:

Some OECD countries have much more equitable policies regulating school admission than others, and sorting of students by proficiency levels occurs at a later age. Interventions that aim to bolster both cognitive and non-cognitive skills of students from disadvantaged backgrounds can play an important role in limiting social exclusion and facilitating the task of social policies at a later stage of the individuals' life-course.

(Machin, 2006, p 5)

A sociological focus on the structure and organisation of society suggests that children from disadvantaged backgrounds have often been marginalised within UK education systems (eg Ball, 2006). In trying to explain the causes and persistence of poverty in the UK, sociologists often attempt to understand the balance between the organisation of society and the extent to which individuals have choices or control over their lives. In the USA, for example, studies have shown that structural failings in one of the richest nations in the world have resulted in the widening of inequalities and poverty (eg Rank, Yoon and Hirschl, 2003).

There has been much debate among sociologists between those who have tended to blame the victims by referring to dependency cultures or character failings (views perhaps most prevalent in the 1970s and 1980s but which resurface periodically) and those who argue that poverty is a result of unequal distribution of resources across society (see Shildrick and Rucell, 2015). Recent sociological perspectives on poverty suggest that in the UK:

» *social class and processes of class reproduction remain important, particularly for the continuity of poverty over time and across generations;*

» *it is important to understand the stigma and shame in the experience of poverty. A particular concern is with how the spending patterns of those in the greatest poverty are often subject to stigmatization;*

>   » *the ways in which institutions such as public or welfare delivery services can negatively stereotype those experiencing poverty has also been shown to be important in stigmatising and disadvantaging those experiencing poverty;*

>   » *to a large extent, people's social class positions still influence the opportunities open to them. Starting out life in poverty means a greater risk of poverty in later life.*

(Shildrick and Rucell, 2015, p 1)

These findings suggest the importance of avoiding stigmatising both those children living in poverty and the working-class communities in which they live. It also suggests the importance of understanding the many social environments that young people experience in their lives.

Poverty and special educational needs and disability (SEND)

Research has shown that poverty is both a cause and effect of SEND (Shaw et al., 2016). SEND are more prevalent among disadvantaged pupils than among their less disadvantaged peers. Of the pupils eligible for free school meals in England in 2015, 28.7 per cent were identified as having SEND (DfE, 2015). Figures in Northern Ireland, Scotland and Wales also show that a high proportion of those with SEND live in poverty.

The DfE definition of SEND included children with some or all of the following impairments to learning:

>   » *behaviour or ability to socialise (for example, not being able to make friends);*
>   » *reading and writing (for example, they have dyslexia);*
>   » *ability to understand things;*
>   » *concentration levels (for example, they have ADHD);*
>   » *physical needs or impairments.*

(DfE, 2015, p 2)

As mentioned in the previous chapter, it is difficult and sometimes unwise to generalise about children with SEND. Indeed the government change from the use of SEN to SEND in 2014 can be seen as confusing as not all children with a disability have a learning SEN. Of course many pupils do have both special educational needs and a disability of some kind (Parsons and Platt, 2013) and there is considerable overlap in the pupils identified in each category.

Nevertheless, the evidence suggests that living in poverty can make children more susceptible to both special needs and some forms of disability. Evidence for this comes from the fact that the proportion of children with SEND living in poverty increases with age for all types of SEND (Shaw et al., 2016). There are two major reasons for this as:

1. *children who live in poverty are more likely than their affluent peers to develop some forms of SEND, such as behavioural difficulties, as they experience 'persistently challenging family circumstances';*

2. *the families of children with SEND are more likely to move into poverty (for example, as a result of the costs and/or family stress associated with their child's SEND status pushing them into poverty).*

(Shaw et al., 2016, p 9)

Evidence has shown that high-quality teaching of pupils with SEND is vital to both their academic success and well-being in school (Machin, 2006). Schools need to have both classroom teachers who are able to support pupils with SEND in the classroom, and have specialist provision available when needed. Arguably, there is also a benefit for non-SEND low-prior attainers if they are taught by teachers skilled in supporting pupils with SEND (Machin, 2006). However, research suggests that many experienced teachers are not confident in their understanding of SEND, particularly in the area of language impairment (see Chapter 4 for a more complete discussion of the links between language and disadvantage). For example, a study of experienced educational practitioners in the UK showed that many were challenged by the terminology associated with children with speech, language and communication needs (SLCN) (Dockrell and Howell, 2015). In addition, many found difficulties in distinguishing children with SLCN from children with English as an additional language.

There is a need then for professional development for teachers and pre-service teachers in the teaching of children with SEND. In addition, a report for the Joseph Rowntree Foundation recommends that:

» *policy-makers and school and early years leaders should prioritise SEND;*

» *staff in schools and early years settings should be trained to identify needs so that they can be spotted early and over-identification and under-identification are reduced;*

» *targeted funding for pupils with SEND who are at risk of exclusion should be provided so that schools can support them before they are excluded.*

(Shaw et al., 2016, pp 34–35)

Social learning in the classroom

There is a considerable body of research in the field of education that suggests that learning can best be described as a social activity and that learning is mediated both by our contact with others and through the psychological tools that the learners acquire (Claxton, 2007; Mercer, 2000; Vygotsky, 1987). As learning is social, then attention needs to be paid to the social settings in which pupils learn. As pupils from disadvantaged backgrounds are more likely to experience social problems than their peers and be disaffected from learning, the challenge for schools and teachers is to find ways to integrate these young people in the social learning in the classroom.

Mercer (2000), writing from a sociocultural theoretical perspective, highlights the importance of teaching and of organising classroom talk. He identifies three features that good teachers do when they teach well.

1. *They use question-and-answer sequences not just to test knowledge, but also to guide the development of understanding.*

2. *They teach not just 'subject knowledge', but also procedures for solving problems and making sense of experience.*

3. *They treat learning as a 'social, communicative process'.*

(Mercer, 2000, p 160)

In other words, good teaching is as much to do with the social processes of pupils' learning as it is to do with the learning outcomes of the lesson. Teaching higher order skills of problem solving and meaning making means thinking carefully about both task design in lessons and the social organisation of the classroom. Task design relates to the ways that teachers view and use the pedagogic potential of different tasks to engage pupils with knowledge in different subjects (Thompson, 2015). This involves the goal or purpose of the task, the resources available in a given setting and the forms of instruction and intervention that allow pupils to process the information as they negotiate the task activities.

Bruner (1960) argued that learning is facilitated through organised and structured learning experiences and that children need to be provided with opportunities to extend their current understanding. For Bruner, the purpose of education is not simply to impart knowledge, but instead to facilitate children's symbolic thinking and problem-solving skills, which can then be transferred to a range of situations. Bruner also argued that extrinsic rewards should be reduced as learners build expertise and self-motivation. Others have argued that teachers should make learning meaningful and interesting in order to promote long-term retention of knowledge and intrinsic motivation for pupils (Brown, 2007). This means actively teaching a range of learning strategies and encouraging communication among pupils.

Vygotsky (1987) also conceived learning as being both a social and situated cultural activity. Learning involves mediated activity through psychological tool usage and in particular the culturally acquired conceptual tool of language. It therefore matters who we learn from and with, how we learn and where we learn. For Vygotsky, real learning is that which is in advance of development and is mediated through interactions with other people and through the social and cultural acquisition of sign systems. His concept of the zone of proximal development (ZPD), the difference between what a child is able to do with and without help, indicates both the presence of maturing psychological functions and the possibility of meaningful interventions that can stimulate conceptual development. This process of conceptual development involves co-operation and collaboration between the teacher and the learner, or between learners at different levels of development.

Designing the classroom environment

For Bruner and Vygotsky collaboration and co-operation are also crucial features of effective teaching. Vygotsky (1987) argued that learning can take place within a social situation of development when the learning task is set at a level in advance of the student's current mental level of development. This has pedagogic design implications for classroom teachers and teacher educators concerning the relationship between instruction, pupils' development and the classroom environment. Vygotsky argued that school learning introduces something fundamentally new into pupils' development. By giving pupils specific tasks of understanding scientific concepts within a designed environment, school learning introduces new concepts that can in turn stimulate psychological development. It is within the dialectical interplay between the pupils' grasp of everyday or spontaneous concepts and the development of their scientific conceptual understanding that learning leads to development.

However, simply giving pupils tasks or allowing them to communicate does not guarantee learning, particularly for those pupils who are most resistant because of previous negative experiences. As Derry (2008) points out, *the learning environment must be designed and cannot rely on the spontaneous response to an environment which is not constructed according to, or involves, some clearly worked out conceptual framework'* (p 61). In an educational context, while learners' needs must determine classroom activity it is through appropriately structured activity that pupils learn.

In culturally diverse classrooms in the UK, activities of writing, reading, and speaking and listening are both distributed in the sense of many participants contributing to these specific acts of literacy and situated within the context of the classroom and school environment. However, young people with social, emotional and behavioural difficulties often struggle within the performative expectations and cultures of traditional schooling. This leaves them at risk of marginalisation and social exclusion with long-term negative future consequences for their social engagement in the wider world. Success in both academic and emotional terms in secondary school requires self-regulation, emotional resilience and the ability to collaborate with both peers and adults (eg Claxton, 2007). However, the academic demands of the school curriculum allow little time and resources for the development of these psychological and emotional skills or tools.

Claxton (2007) has argued that teachers need to actively create stretching environments for their learners. In particular, Claxton argues that teachers should think about the learning environment, or epistemic culture, that they offer their pupils. These cultures may be prohibiting, affording, inviting or potentiating. However, only potentiating environments actually stretch learners. Claxton explains that:

Only the fourth kind of epistemic culture, potentiating milieux, make the exercise of learning muscles both appealing and challenging. In a potentiating environment, there are plenty of hard, interesting things to do, and it is accepted as normal that everyone regularly gets confused, frustrated and stuck.

(Claxton, 2007, p 125)

Claxton's metaphor of 'learning muscles' for higher order thinking skills comes from his analogy of teachers being fitness instructors in a gym who help their pupils to 'build learning power'.

Pupil grouping and resourcing

Creating a positive climate for learning for socially disadvantaged pupils means thinking carefully about both how pupils are grouped and what school resources are used to support them. Research has shown that school decisions about pupil grouping and resourcing can have a profound impact on pupils from disadvantaged backgrounds. For example, low-income pupils are most likely to make significant progress in secondary schools that specifically focus on low-income pupils' progress, both in terms of setting and sharing high expectations for pupils (Shaw et al., 2017). Low-income pupils are less likely to make good progress in schools where they are grouped by ability from an early age, and where resources are concentrated on Key Stage 4 instead of younger pupils (Machin, 2006). This is particularly important when pupils are transitioning from primary to secondary school. Some Organisation for Economic Co-operation and Development (OECD) countries have much more equitable policies than England on regulating school admission (Machin, 2006). In many of these countries the sorting of students by proficiency levels occurs at a later age if at all.

Assessing pupils' progress in the classroom

Assessing pupils' progress is a key part of a teacher's job. Without reprising the arguments for assessment *for* learning as opposed to assessment *of* learning (see Black and Wiliam, 2005) in detail, it is worth reiterating the point that assessment should be about helping pupils to develop and progress in their learning. Vadeboncoeur (2017) points out that for Vygotsky what should matter for teachers are measures of relative achievement, or how much they have improved from earlier achievement. Measuring absolute achievement by comparing one student to another provides little information relevant to the learning of a particular pupil. School data are helpful for assessment, and many successful schools use data analysis both to track progress and to intervene swiftly and flexibly when pupils do not make progress. But this progress should be relative for each pupil rather than identifying particular members of a cohort who might improve a school's position in the league tables.

In a review of written marking and assessment in UK primary and secondary schools, Elliott et al. (2016) point out the dangers of excessive written marking, which can lead to demoralisation particularly for those pupils who most struggle with writing. For example, they point out that careless mistakes should be marked differently to errors resulting from misunderstanding. The former might be addressed by simply marking the mistake as incorrect, without giving the right answer, while the advice for errors is to provide hints or questions which lead pupils to underlying principles. Of course this means that the teacher needs to have a good understanding of the current ability of their pupils. Continuous assessment of all pupils is fundamental to addressing social disadvantage as this ensures both that all pupils needs can be met and that weaker pupils are not singed out. Elliott et al. advise that:

> » *awarding grades for every piece of work may reduce the impact of marking, particularly if pupils become preoccupied with grades at the expense of a consideration of teachers' formative comments;*

>> *the use of targets to make marking as specific and actionable as possible is likely to increase pupil progress;*

>> *pupils are unlikely to benefit from marking unless some time is set aside to enable pupils to consider and respond to marking;*

>> *some forms of marking, including acknowledgement marking, are unlikely to enhance pupil progress. A mantra might be that schools should mark less in terms of the number of pieces of work marked, but mark better.*

(Elliott et al., 2016, p 3)

The role of emotion and imagination

Far too many young people find themselves on the margins of education or socially excluded from their peers. Both secondary and primary schools report that many of their pupils struggle to cope with the twin demands of a results-driven education system and the difficult transitions that they have to negotiate in their personal and social lives. Much of the research suggests that marginalisation in education has negative long-term consequences for young people in terms of social engagement in the wider world, academic attainment, emotional development and future employment (Stamou et al., 2014). Arguably, many of these young people become estranged from forms of schooling that they find difficult to navigate.

Vygotsky (1993) identified emotional experience, or the young person's affective relationship to their environment, as the key unit of analysis for an understanding of their development. Vygotsky perceived imagination, cognition and emotion as being closely interrelated. He argued that imagination in adolescence is the successor of children's play and plays a key role in their development. Imagination, invoked through the social situation of play and mediated through interaction with others, can help a young person to change their perceptions about the imagined worlds of the future. Research has shown that arts-based interventions can be effective for some young people in certain circumstances (eg Elliott and Dingwall, 2017; Thompson and Tawell, 2017) and that arts participation is a potentially important foundation for well-rounded child and adolescent development (see Chapter 5).

Vygotsky (1993) showed that child development involves periods of crisis, or critical periods, as the learner encounters contradictions between their own current psychological development and the new demands of different learning situations. When there is a clash between the personal and social (the potential crisis point), a young person, through interaction with others, can begin to envisage things in a new way. However, these social situations of development can lead to considerable frustration for disadvantaged young people who are socially isolated. Thompson and Tawell (2017) have argued that at adolescence, this frustration can also lead to clashes with the authority and views of parenting or schooling as the young person develops a more critical understanding of cultural and social norms that they had previously accepted.

Within schools, the remedy offered to those who struggle to engage with an academic curriculum has traditionally been to offer more of what has failed in the first place, particularly in the areas of English, or literacy, and mathematics. However, there is a growing recognition that emotion and imagination are central aspects in the development both in very young children (eg Fleer and Hammer, 2013) and in adolescence (eg Hughes and Wilson, 2004). Evoking play through storytelling, drama, music or a range of other artistic activities can help young people's ability to self-regulate, empathise with others and work collaboratively. Arguably, developing these attributes is key to young people's self-esteem and their ability, in turn, to tackle curriculum areas that they have found problematic.

Tackling social disadvantage through research

Supporting the learning and well-being of disadvantaged pupils is an important yet challenging part of school educators' work. It is also crucial that teachers collaborate with each other and share strategies and advice on how to support disadvantaged groups and individuals. In a report from the Social Mobility Commission, it was found that school culture is important for disadvantaged pupils (Shaw et al., 2017). Collaborative schools with pedagogically skilled staff who believe that low-income pupils are capable of making as much relative progress as their more affluent peers are more likely to succeed in tackling the inequities of social disadvantage. Research in this field shows that interventions that involve teachers taking a collective responsibility for students' well-being and attainment, through collaboration that is focused on their students' learning, are effective in supporting the progress of vulnerable learners (eg Goddard, Goddard and Tschannen-Moran, 2007). The final section of this chapter looks at a research project that attempted to map collaborative patterns in secondary schools with teaching practices most associated with helping disadvantaged pupils.

Teacher collaboration to support vulnerable learners

The two-phase study *Collaboration for Effective Teaching and Learning*, conducted in the academic years 2014–15 and 2015–16, investigated variations in patterns of collaboration among professional staff in six English secondary schools within an ethnically mixed city in the south-east region of England with wide disparities between areas of wealth and poverty. The schools selected reflect the local diversity as they differ in terms of overall levels of academic performance and serve communities with different deprivation levels.

Phase one of the study used a mixed methods approach that combined findings from Social Network Analysis (SNA) with in-depth interviews in order to understand social networks and staff perceptions of schools' climate for collaboration. This SNA data collection involved an extensive online survey which was sent to 484 teachers working in the six participant schools that asked respondents to indicate who they went to for advice on working with disadvantaged pupils and the frequency of interactions. The instrument covered several background characteristics, including: gender; the number of years each spent working in schools in general and in their current school in particular; perceptions of school climate for collaboration; and frequency and impact of collaboration with other colleagues in their school. A satisfactory average response rate of 90 per cent, with a range of 81–98 per cent, was obtained. Data were also collected using semi-structured interviews in each school with the headteacher, the special needs coordinator (SENCO) and two classroom teachers. These interviews helped to triangulate the results obtained from the SNA quantitative analysis, as well as to identify the types of informal collaborative practices that take place in the sample schools and their perceived impact on teacher practice and vulnerable students' learning and well-being. Teachers with a high degree of centrality to the social network were those most frequently nominated by their peers as someone they went to for advice on supporting disadvantaged pupils.

The key findings of phase one were that:

» schools with networks that extend beyond departmental silos were more effective in supporting vulnerable learners' attainment and well-being;

» school culture had a significant effect on patterns of collaboration;

» some teachers in schools, other than the SENCO, had high degrees of centrality in the social networks.

Phase two explored the relationship between teachers' patterns of collaboration, their teaching practices and their pupils' levels of engagement in lessons by addressing the research question: to what extent are teachers who are highly central to the collaboration networks of their schools more likely to show teaching practices associated with teacher effectiveness than less networked educators?

Twenty-two teachers were identified from the school that had the highest density of network activity (the most reciprocal patterns of advice seeking), high levels of deprivation among its pupils and a high proportion of EAL learners. The teachers chosen ranged from the highest to the least central and came from a wide range of subjects. The researchers used different observation tools which focused on the teachers' practices and the response of disadvantaged pupils, respectively. All pupils in Year 9 were asked to complete the School Connectedness Survey and the Strengths and Difficulties Questionnaire (widely used brief assessments of well-being and engagement).

The findings from this phase showed a clear link between strong teacher collaboration and effective teaching practice in that teachers who were most central in the networks were most likely to use pedagogic techniques associated with effective teaching. The strongest correlations were that:

» students were actively engaged in learning;

» the teacher presented the lesson with a logical flow that moves from simple to more complex concepts;

» the teacher managed the lesson smoothly moving from one stage to another with well-managed transition points;

» the teacher encouraged students to ask one another questions and to explain their understanding of topics to one other;

» the teacher demonstrated genuine warmth and empathy towards all students in the classroom;

» the teacher created purposeful activities that engage every student in productive work;

» the teacher's instruction was interactive (lots of questions and answers).

It is also interesting to note that the length of service as a teacher was not a factor in the centrality of teachers. Newly qualified teachers were just as likely to both seek and give advice and to use effective pedagogy as their more experienced peers. These findings suggest that changing the culture of collaborative practices is an important step in meeting the needs of disadvantaged pupils.

IN A **NUTSHELL**

Poverty, SEND and other forms of social disadvantage can have deeply harmful educational and psychological consequences for the cognitive, emotional and social development of children. The negative effects of social and economic disadvantage on cognition begin early in life and continue to grow through the school years. In order to address the question of how to tackle social disadvantage in the classroom, teachers and teacher educators need to consider the cognitive, affective and social processes involved in learning. Research has shown that teacher collaboration can help in addressing social disadvantage.

REFLECTIONS ON **CRITICAL ISSUES**

• *Social disadvantage can have damaging cognitive and affective consequences for children, leading to developmental delay.*

• *Social disadvantage is strongly associated with psychological, environmental and sociological factors.*

• *Schools and classroom teachers do need to address the cognitive and affective consequences of poverty and social disadvantage on children and their learning.*

• *Research has shown that effective teacher collaboration can help them to support vulnerable learners.*

CRITICAL **ISSUES**

- *What are some common misconceptions held by teachers of the effects of poverty and disadvantage on children and their learning and educational achievement and why are these views so hard to change?*

- *What effect do these misconceptions have on the learning opportunities for children living in poverty?*

- *What are some of the social and economic realities for young people living in poverty?*

- *What can research tell us about ways to challenge and change some teachers' misconceptions of poverty and educational achievement?*

The pedagogy of poverty

Child poverty is a cause of major concern for schools and teachers. The link between poverty and poor educational outcomes is well documented as have been the effects of poverty on young peoples' health and well-being. As Horgan (2007) has pointed out, children's experience of schooling is largely determined by the level of disadvantage that they face in their life both in and out of school. However, not all pupils from impoverished backgrounds struggle at school and there is some research evidence to suggest that teachers who are responsive to the particular needs of disadvantaged students can make a difference (eg Thrupp, Mansell, Hawksworth, and Harold, 2003). Unfortunately, some relatively rare examples of successful schools serving high-poverty communities are sometimes used to claim that low achievement in other schools is entirely the fault of the teachers working in them, without examining their specific circumstances or contexts. At the same time there is evidence that negative stereotypes held by some new and established teachers about impoverished children can perpetuate inequality (eg Gorski, 2012; Smyth and Wrigley, 2013; Thompson, McNicholl and Menter, 2016).

Teachers making a difference

Virtually all teachers come into the profession wanting to make a difference to the lives of the young people they will teach. These teachers are by very definition committed to improving the learning opportunities for all the young people in their care. Teachers also have an important pastoral role in supporting the emotional well-being of their students within the school environment. In the primary school sector, teachers spend a significant amount of time with their class and can become receptive to subtle changes in the motivation and concentration levels of their pupils. Secondary school teachers, by contrast, teach a large number of children of different ages. The amount of daily contact they have with these children depends in part on their subject specialism and the timetabling of curriculum provision. Nevertheless, most secondary teachers also have pastoral roles in supporting their tutor group. Assessing students' emotional and material needs, and allocating the valuable and pressured resource of teacher time necessary to support students in need, is just one of the many considerations in the daily life of teaching.

For students from disadvantaged and impoverished backgrounds, the role of the teacher may be of critical importance. Disadvantaged students spend a considerable amount of time in school and this experience may be a relatively stable and safe one compared to the chaos imposed by conditions of poverty. Ridge (2009) has reported that whilst the school environment represents a crucial area for potential intervention to improve the lives of low-income and disadvantaged children, many of these children feel very negatively about their school experience. Many children living in poverty perceive that some teachers have very low academic expectations of them because of their social and economic background. They may also feel that teachers do not respect them, their parents or carers, or even the area in which they live. This belief can be substantiated through conversations in many school staffrooms where the frustration of teachers and support staff may be articulated in casual stereotypes of children from particular estates or backgrounds.

The consequences of testing and performativity

So where does this disconnect between teachers wanting to make a difference and the negative perceptions of disadvantaged students come from? One reason is the constant pressure on teachers to perform both in judgments of their pedagogic practice and the outcomes and progress of their students. Performativity demands, league tables based on published examination results, and the threat of imminent school inspection often dominates the discourse and practice of schools and teachers. As a result, despite teachers being fully aware of their combined academic and pastoral role, many feel their primary responsibility to be the academic progress and attainment of their students. Performance management and numerical targets inevitably mean a disproportionate amount of time can be spent on teaching the children on grade borderlines rather than those necessarily in need of extra attention because of social and economic disadvantage. Indeed, one of the inevitable consequences of the high-stakes testing in schools that is designed to hold schools and teachers accountable (Furlong and Lunt, 2014) is a restriction of the curriculum for disadvantaged children.

The pressures on schools to introduce measures for their students to pass the next test may be at the expense of strategies that assist young people's long-term cognitive development or emotional well-being. In primary schools in England the pressure on schools to achieve high scores in standardised attainment tests (SATS) inevitably results in pressure on disadvantaged students despite the efforts of teachers to protect them. In secondary schools issues such as setting and ability grouping go largely unquestioned and 'pedagogies of poverty', based on transmission of knowledge and teacher control, are reinforced (Smyth and Wrigley, 2013). As Haberman (1991) pointed out long ago, the problem with the pedagogy of poverty in urban schools is that it does not work. Instruction becomes ritualised and resented by both learners and their teachers who battle to maintain authority. An over-emphasis on basic skills in this model inevitably is at the expense of higher order skills of conceptual understanding, critical thinking, problem solving or creativity. The irony is that even basic skills are not taught effectively through this model. For disadvantaged students, this may mean that any interventions offered are simply repetitions of the techniques that had failed to help or engage them in the first place.

Another reason for the disconnection between teachers' intentions to support impoverished learners and the negative experiences of these students may be that many teachers lack personal knowledge and understanding of the effects of poverty. Teachers come into the profession as a result of academic success and are statistically more likely to have come from relatively stable economic backgrounds. Lack of personal experience of poverty may be compounded for some teachers by a lack of teaching opportunities in urban schools during their initial teacher education. What little knowledge some teachers have of poverty is often misinformed and based on stereotypical assumptions. Of course this is not true of all teachers, but this is of no comfort to those disadvantaged students whose learning in school is mediated through a teacher with misconceptions of the effects of poverty. Before we focus on what these misconceptions are, and how they might be changed, it is necessary at this point to outline the complex links between poverty and education as well as some of the economic and social realities of life for young people living in poverty.

Poverty, educational attainment and well-being

It would be wrong to generalise about social disadvantage in education. Poverty affects children to different degrees and in many complex ways. Poverty is a relative term but it is also a very broad term with much dispute about definition. For example in the UK, the receipt of free school meals is often used as a proxy measure for poverty. In fact the measure is highly problematic due to its narrow scope, diminishing claims and incomplete take-up. The now universal free school meals (FSM) for infant children (5- to 7-year-olds) in the UK will further complicate this issue. In the year 2015–16 the Department for Education (DfE) reported that the proportion of children on FSM fell to 14.3 per cent (down from 18 per cent in 2012) whilst the Child Poverty Action Group reported figures from the Department for Work and Pensions, which showed official child poverty figures in 2014–15 had risen by 200,000 in a year to 3.9 million children. This represents 28 per cent of all children in the UK or nine in a typical classroom of 30.

What is not in dispute is the seriousness of the problem of child poverty and the potential damage to the well-being and educational attainment of these students in schools. Statistically, children from impoverished backgrounds do worse than their more privileged peers at all stages of education from early assessments in literacy and numeracy, through compulsory and post-compulsory schooling, and in further or higher education. These children are also more likely to face permanent or fixed-term exclusions from school, exhibit mental health problems, and suffer long-term employment problems as adults. Even given the imperfection of FSM as a measure of poverty, the attainment gap between FSM students and their peers is significant. Nationally available data shows that the gap is present when children enter schooling and widens as they move through the school system (Strand, 2014). In England, the gap exists in almost all schools, even those rated 'outstanding' by England's inspection body, Ofsted (Strand 2014).

> » The FSM attainment gap in Key Stage 1 mathematics increased from 8 to 18 percentage points in 2016, when the tests were made more complex.

> » Students with FSM are almost half as likely to achieve five or more A*–C GCSE grades including English and mathematics than other pupils (33 per cent compared to 61 per cent in 2015).

> » Compared to their peers, students with FSM entitlement only have around a quarter the chance of achieving A or A* grades at GCSE level.

The Sutton Trust reports that of students in the poorest fifth of the population who, against the national trend, were in the top fifth of national attainment at age 11, two-thirds were no longer in the top fifth at age 16 and only around one in seven proceeded to university (Sutton Trust, 2008). Crawford et al. (2016) highlight recent statistics that show that:

> » *only 24% of young people from the poorest fifth of areas enter university, compared with 60% from the most prosperous;*

> » *22% of young people from the richest fifth of the population get a place at one of the 24 Russell Group universities, but only 2% from the poorest fifth.*

As Ball (2006) has repeatedly and eloquently argued, the systems of education in the UK are class based and favour those middle and upper-class families who have the cultural and financial resources to navigate the system in support of their children.

Extremes of poverty across the UK are an increasingly worrying feature. In a recent Joseph Rowntree study, Bramley et al. (2016) found that some 300,000 children in the UK lived in destitution at some point in 2015, affecting one in 20 households in some areas. The major reasons behind child destitution were identified as: a benefit sanction or delay; sudden high household bills; unemployment; or family breakdown. The social and emotional consequences for the young people involved are both evident as well as complex and individual. The social stigma attached to poverty means that schools and teachers may be unaware of major changes in young people's lives that significantly affect their ability to concentrate academically and to interact and socialise with peers and adults.

Rural child poverty is also a significant factor across the UK. Whilst the proportion of poorer children is statistically smaller, these children and their families often lack access to the appropriate support systems. Indeed, in England the attainment of disadvantaged children tends to be lower where such children constitute a minority of the school population (Strand, 2014). One explanation might be that they become 'invisible' within the larger, economically more advantaged, population. Children and families living in rural areas often lack access to the resources available to their urban counterparts. However, the fact that these children fare worse also implies that teachers and schools can have an impact on the poverty attainment gap. Indeed, another implication of the particular lack of progress of poor children in rural areas may be that their teachers lack the expertise and knowledge to intervene and help them effectively. It is also clear that all teachers in state schools will teach significant numbers of children living in poverty in their careers and that addressing poverty-related attainment is an issue for all educators. As Jensen (2009) and others argue it is essential that teachers develop an understanding of the effects of poverty for the young people in their classrooms.

Some realities for children living in poverty

Ridge (2009), in a review of the literature on children's and families' experiences of poverty, highlights both the economic and material effects of poverty on children and their resultant emotional well-being. Children worry about the inadequacy of income in their household. They may lack what many would regard as essential childhood possessions for their social and cognitive development, such as toys and books, and they are often short of everyday essentials for school. Opportunities at school are often restricted because of an inability to pay for extra resources such as study guides or school trips. Caring and other duties may also mean that after school clubs are not open to them.

'Free schooling' in the UK is actually quite expensive when you add up the cost of a uniform, physical education (PE) kit, school bag, coats, lunches, school trips, stationary and curriculum materials. In 2014 the Children's Commission on Poverty found the average annual total cost of schooling in the UK to be around £800 with some schools ignoring guideline and legal requirements on costs. *Households Below Average Income* statistics (2015) show that children from the fifth poorest-income households were 11 times less likely to be able to afford school trips and 20 times less likely to be able to attend an organised activity each week. An additional problem for disadvantaged young people is that their lack of equipment or inability to pay for resources can lead to conflict with teachers and even disciplinary action within the school.

One of the myths about young people living in poverty is that they are passive victims of their fate. In fact, most try to take responsibility and alleviate the strain on family resources. This means that these young people often do not pass on requests for money from schools or keep quiet about elective school trips even when financial assistance is offered by schools. The resilience and varied life experience of these disadvantaged young people means that they also have qualities and particular forms of cultural knowledge that can be drawn on to help their learning. González, Moll and Amanti (2005) have described the 'funds of knowledge' that young people possess from their cultural experiences outside of school that could be drawn on to help them make sense of the school curriculum. As Ridge (2009) argues, children in poverty want to be active members of their school community. They have the same social and cultural expectations and they are motivated by the same social imperatives as others. Of course the visible signs of poverty can mark children out as different. This is most obvious in clothing but also in the lack of other material goods that have symbolic importance to their peers. Indeed, poverty in an affluent area can be particularly isolating and consequently damaging to their social interactions. Moving school is potentially disruptive for all children, but particularly so for those children living in poverty and for those from marginalised backgrounds such as refugee or traveller families. Of course, the current economic crisis, benefit cuts and the increased reliance on private rented accommodation means that more families are likely to face this disruption.

Another myth is that young people from impoverished backgrounds have parents or carers who do not value education. Lister (2004) has argued that mothers in particular bear the brunt of the cost of trying to alleviate the effects of poverty for their children. This can mean enormous personal sacrifice. Ridge (2009) adds that parents living under extreme economic pressure often feel that they have failed to bring up their children adequately. The stigma and social shame of poverty can make parents wary of contact with schools, particularly those who had negative experience of schooling themselves. As noted before, Cummins et al. (2012) found that most young people and parents from impoverished circumstances attached great importance to education and did have realistic aspirations. What they did not have were opportunity, resources and the economic ability to allow their children to experiment.

Poverty proofing the school day

Of course schools and teachers themselves cannot reverse economic patterns of disadvantage and inequality. Besides the need to bring about wider structural change, it is also essential to eradicate exclusionary institutional practices and attitudes. The Children's Commission on Poverty in the UK has recommended that schools adopt 'poverty proofing' measures in order to increase the possibility of making education an inclusive experience for all students. This means assessing the ways that schools deal with extra costs for education and avoiding additional 'voluntary' contributions that put pressure on young people and their families. It also means reducing punitive measures that both stigmatise and blame the child living in poverty. The Commission also recommends that teachers should be offered training to improve their understanding of poverty. The ways that teachers behave and interact with these students both in and out of the classroom can be important. Children North East has developed a toolkit to poverty proof the school day (Mazzoli Smith and Todd, 2016).The toolkit advocates basic methods to prevent poorer students being discriminated against such as: more breakfast clubs; free food and drink before exams; improved IT access; changing the ways in which school meals and uniforms are administered; and cutting the number of non-uniform days.

Deficit views of poverty

Research has shown that some in-service and pre-service teachers lack a critical perspective on the contexts of poverty and social disadvantage and may hold deficit views of students in poverty that suggest these students are unable to learn and need to be controlled. Thompson, McNicholl and Menter (2016) have argued that these views are often entrenched and hard to change. While a number of researchers, particularly in the USA, have consistently considered the role that ITE might have in overcoming social justice inequalities (eg Cochran-Smith, 2004; Zeichner, 2009), remarkably little research exists that directly addresses any linkages between poverty and teacher education.

Some researchers have recently drawn attention to the impact that socio-economic disadvantage can have on young people's life chances (Buras, 2014; Gorski, 2012). Much of this work has sought to critique the 'culture of poverty' that has come to dominate much of the discourse from politicians, the media and, in some cases, educational commentators. Gorski (2012) argues that this 'culture of poverty' is underpinned by a deficit ideology, or deficit thinking, where the perceived shortcomings of the poor, rather than structural inequalities, are used to explain why children who live in economic disadvantage more often than not have poor educational outcomes. Buras (2014) points out the link between the 'culture of poverty' and the neo-conservative argument that children living in poverty lack the necessary dispositions and cultural assets to do well in school. Researchers in England (eg Dorling, 2011; Smyth and Wrigley, 2013; Thompson, McNicholl and Menter, 2016) have also argued that blaming impoverished students and their families for poor educational outcomes is a failure to understand the effects of poverty and risks the danger of blaming young people. As Dudley-Marling and Lucas (2009) stress, ignoring the positive possibilities that cultural and linguistic diversity brings to classrooms leads to the pathologising of poor children and their language and culture. Negative stereotypes about impoverished children based on assumptions of low educational aspirations can also perpetuate inequality (Cummings et al., 2012).

Gorski (2012) argues that in comparison to indicators of factors affecting educational attainment, such as ethnicity or gender, there is less clarity about the impact of socio-economic class. Gorski suggests that the combination of deficit ideologies and misunderstandings of the economic and social realities of poverty represent an issue of ignorance about the lives of 'others'. In these conditions the tendency is 'to imagine our own social and cultural identity groups as diverse while we imagine "the other" people belonging to a social or cultural identity group with which we are less familiar, as being, for all intents and purposes, monolithic' (Gorski, 2012, pp 302–3). The danger is that this imagining without knowledge about certain groups or communities leads us to 'use stereotypes to fill in the blanks' (Gorski, 2012, p 303). Rank, Yoon and Hirschl (2003) argue that many people, including established and beginning teachers, not only believe people are poor because of their own deficiencies but also hold other stereotypical views about pupils and their families. These views might include believing that poor parents do not value education and that students do not achieve because they are either lazy or lack the intellectual capacity to learn. This 'deficit ideology', or 'culture of poverty' (Ladson-Billings, 2006), leads some teachers to define 'the problem in terms of students' inabilities to achieve and their families' inability to help them achieve rather than the many barriers that impede their achievement' (Gorski, 2012, pp 313–14). The pervasiveness of such deficit thinking and stereotyping, even among those teachers and students apparently committed to educational equality, can lead to low expectations of students from impoverished backgrounds.

Social justice and ITE

Social justice agendas theoretically underpin many ITE programmes around the world (Zeichner, 2009), including those in the UK, the aim being to prepare teachers who are capable of teaching all pupils, not just those who have been traditionally well served by schools. However, Schwartz (1996) pointed out over 20 years ago in the context of New York schools the *'disquieting and undeniable reality is that novice teachers are not adequately prepared by their colleges and universities for the classroom experiences found in typical city schools'* (p 82). The implication that teachers can only learn about the lives of children living in poverty from direct experience has partly fuelled the rise of employment-based routes such as Teach for America and Teach First in England. However, the apprenticeship models of these and other routes, with a decreased higher education influence, stands in stark contrast to the practical theorising approach of clinical practice models (see Burn, Hagger and Mutton, 2015; Hagger and McIntyre, 2006). The clinical practice approach stresses both the dialectical interplay between theories of education and teaching practice as well as the developmental importance of disrupting and questioning previous assumptions about pedagogy and the ways particular people learn in particular circumstances.

Moreover, reviews of the teacher education literature provide strong evidence that beginning teachers' pre-existing beliefs shape their ITE experience and these views are remarkably resistant to change (eg Lupton and Thrupp, 2013; Thompson, McNicholl and Menter 2015). Many teachers do indeed hold stereotypical ideas about pupils and parents and consequently locate the causes of educational underachievement due to poverty within the pupil or the home rather than within institutional structures and practices. Other teachers may feel powerless to challenge the stereotypical views of others or to affect the internal logic of a performance-driven curriculum. Real change requires a thorough overhaul of the values and curriculum and systemic change of the kind envisaged by Ball (2006), Zeichner (2009) and others. Yet as the issue of child poverty is critical to educational social justice agendas, and children are facing these issues now, it would be immoral not to try to improve their educational experience though tackling the hard-to-change views and misconceptions of some teachers.

Challenging deficit views of poverty through research

So how can deficit models be challenged through teacher education? Research suggests that teacher education programmes and schools can challenge some entrenched views through:

- » professional development programmes;
- » practical changes to the school environment that help to 'poverty proof' children's experiences; and
- » exposure to relevant theory through reading relevant research and policy literature.

Two examples of research conducted in two contrasting parts of the UK serve here to illustrate both the difficulties and possibilities for challenging and potentially changing entrenched views. The research took place in very different contexts: a secondary school ITE course in Oxford, England and a primary school ITE course in Strathclyde, Scotland. Common concerns of the research studies were questions of how student teachers understand the effect of poverty on pupils' educational achievement, and what they as prospective teachers can do to effect change. The Oxford study illustrates the problematic issue of student teachers' perceptions of poverty, whilst the Strathclyde data suggest the potential power of a focused intervention. The policy and practice implications of these research projects and the contrasts between them has been documented in full elsewhere (Ellis et al., 2016). Here the focus is on the implications of the findings from these studies.

Oxford case study

The Oxford study investigated ways that secondary trainee teachers' views on poverty were subjected to challenge and change during an initial teacher education course in England. This mixed methods study highlighted some of the difficulties faced by teacher educators in challenging entrenched views on poverty and educational attainment. The methods involved pre- and post-course surveys that examined the trainees' beliefs and attitudes to poverty and educational attainment. The intervention involved a series of provocations such as course readings and a lecture on issues of poverty and educational achievement that was delivered to the whole cohort immediately after the first survey in order to challenge perceptions of poverty and educational attainment. The trainees were subsequently asked to reflect on the discussions in the light of their school experience in two placements on the course. In a second stage (a second survey and focus group interviews), the aim was both to gauge trainee teachers' perceptions of poverty and also to determine what influence various aspects of the course had had on their beliefs such as placement schools, school mentors, university tutors, university sessions or working directly with parents and students.

In the Oxford study the focus was on exploring trainee teachers' perceptions of poverty and educational achievement. A pre-course survey asked the cohort of trainee teachers ($n=185$) to respond to a series of questions about their perceptions of poverty and educational achievement. Eighty-two per cent described themselves coming from middle- to high-income backgrounds. When the trainee teachers were asked what had the largest impact on pupils' educational outcomes, life choice and opportunities the results were: Parents'/Carers' Attitudes to Education, 81 per cent; Social Class, 8 per cent; Income Levels, 7 per cent; Gender, 3 per cent. The vast majority of the cohort therefore seemed to hold deficit views about children in poverty by blaming attitudes rather than economic and social conditions.

The second survey ($n=179$), conducted at the end of the course, began by asking the trainee teachers whether they agreed with the following assertion: 'There is a link between poverty and pupils' educational outcomes, life choices and opportunities' ($n=166$). The finding that

24 per cent at the end of an ITE course disagreed that there was a link between poverty and educational achievement was a revealing finding for a course that had repeatedly made this link explicit through the sharing of research findings in university- and school-based sessions. It can also be argued that the majority of the 76 per cent of the trainees who did believe there was a link between poverty and educational attainment fell back on deficit models for their interpretation of why this should be the case. One hundred and eighteen comments on the reasons for the given answers on these questions were coded for four different factors: parental deficit (41 per cent); pupil deficit (19.5 per cent); school factors (positive and negative) (7.5 per cent); and socio-economic factors (32 per cent).

The conclusion drawn from this study was that entrenched views are hard to change without direct participation of students from impoverished backgrounds and teachers with experience of working to alleviate the effects of poverty for these youngsters. The social justice agenda of the course, and direct input from both university and school educators, had some effect in changing student teachers' perceptions through discussion and explication. However, 40 per cent of the cohort did not change their views. The prompts and provocations were ultimately relatively weak levers for change. The provocative lecture had the most effect but this did not break into the hard-to-reach perceptions of many of the trainees. The majority held deficit models of young people and families in poverty at the start and end of the course, and even those that accepted the correlation between poverty and educational outcomes blamed the parents or a lack of imagination or ambition within the child. Simply being told that this was not true had little to no impact.

Strathclyde case study

The Strathclyde Literacy Clinic study was an intervention that operated in schools based in one of the poorest parts of Glasgow. The study was designed to potentially re-shape trainee teachers' beliefs about children who live in poverty and their own role in relation to challenging inequality. The data were collected over two years from two separate student cohorts and the entire data-set consists of: the trainee teachers' written notes and reflections whilst working in the clinic; in-depth semi-structured interviews conducted towards the end of their clinic; and written reflections after clinic work had finished. About 80 ITE primary school trainees participated annually, working in teaching teams of four for 10 weeks with one child aged 7–10 years who had struggled to learn to read. The data sources revealed a profound change in most of the trainee teachers' understandings of life in disadvantaged families and of how poverty impacts educational attainment in the context of schooling. This was so regardless of the trainee teachers' past placements in schools serving deprived areas or personal experiences of growing up in such areas. The evidence that emerged was that, after an initial stage of dislocation and, for some, shock, one-to-one discussions between the trainee teachers and child disrupted the trainee teachers' assumptions about schooling by being confronted with the perspective of the child. They came to understand through this process the ways in which organisational measures, such as within-class attainment groupings, could negatively impact reading choice and enjoyment as well as self-esteem and friendships.

Conclusions

What the findings from both studies make clear is that successfully challenging student teachers' understandings of social justice and equity in education is not just about direct experience. As Ellis et al. (2016) point out, even strong, well-established ITE courses with social justice as a core value cannot simply rely on placement experiences and the views of mentors and other teachers in schools to change long-established patterns of belief. The research presented here shows that changing entrenched ideas also requires input from research and professional literature, research provocations and collaborative challenge developed in different contexts of use. Student teachers need to understand the ways in which complex social factors such as home, community and school circumstances as well as affective and personal factors can combine in different ways to impact on learning.

The Oxford intervention shows that whilst ITE courses can successfully challenge some preconceptions, there are significant limitations to simply telling trainee teachers what to believe. If trainee teachers hold entrenched deficit models that essentially blame the learner then a disruption or dislocation through direct or reported experience may be required to change these seemingly fixed views. However, hard to change does not necessarily mean impossible to change and the Strathclyde Literacy Clinic findings suggest that direct experience of working with young learners from impoverished backgrounds in situations outside of normal teaching practice, backed up by reflections on literature and findings from other research studies, can dislocate and change previous assumptions.

These realignments offer tentative hope that, as trainee teachers learn to use different kinds of evidence and different ways of thinking, they can develop new understandings of their role in making schooling more equitable for children living in poverty. Understanding the impact of material conditions on children's learning may be something that beginning and established teachers who do understand the link between poverty and educational achievement feel deeply frustrated about as they cannot by themselves solve the problems of society. Nevertheless, they can be supported in developing an ambitious and critical approach to their teaching based on a commitment to overcoming the impacts of poverty on young people's learning. This means schools devising professional development training that both contextualises the lives of young people living in poverty and refocuses attention on the forms of pedagogy that can help them learn.

IN A **NUTSHELL**

Research has shown that some in-service and pre-service teachers lack a critical perspective on the contexts of poverty and social disadvantage. Some may also hold deficit views of students in poverty where the perceived shortcomings of the poor, rather than structural inequalities, are used to explain why children who live in economic disadvantage more often than not have poor educational outcomes. This culture of poverty suggests that young people living in poverty are unable to learn and need to be controlled. These views are often entrenched and hard to change. These deficit views alongside pressures of performativity can help to perpetuate the pedagogies of poverty. The material and social reality of poverty make it difficult for young people affected to fit in with the culture of schooling despite having similar aims and aspirations as their peers. However, research has shown that in certain circumstances research interventions and professional development programmes can identify and tackle misconceptions of social disadvantage and the effects on educational achievement. Whilst disadvantaged young people may currently lack the cultural and social awareness required for success in education they also have qualities and particular forms of cultural knowledge that can be drawn on by teachers to help their learning. By understanding the causes of poverty, and through poverty proofing the school day, institutions and teachers can make some difference to the learning of disadvantaged young people.

REFLECTIONS ON **CRITICAL ISSUES**

- *Some teachers hold deficit views of learners living in poverty. These views effectively blame the learner, their families or their communities for educational disadvantage. Although these views are hard to change, as they are based on beliefs formed before initial teacher education, they can and should be challenged.*

- *These misconceptions can limit the learning opportunities for children living in poverty through low expectations and a belief that these young people are unable to learn and need to be controlled.*

- *The social and economic realities for young people living in poverty are complex and profound. Poverty can lead to conflict with teachers as well as social and emotional difficulties interacting with peers. However, children living in poverty are not passive victims and they can develop resilient qualities.*

- *Research has shown that in certain circumstances research interventions and professional development programmes can identify and change teachers' misconceptions of social disadvantage and the effects on educational achievement.*

CHAPTER 4 | LANGUAGE, LITERACY AND DISADVANTAGE

CRITICAL **ISSUES**

- *What is the relationship between social disadvantage and language and literacy difficulties?*

- *What is the link between language and literacy difficulties and exclusion from school?*

- *What are some of the short- and long-term consequences of poor language and literacy skills?*

- *What are some possible links between English as an additional language and disadvantage?*

- *How can language across the curriculum policies and practice help disadvantaged pupils?*

Introduction

Many pupils from disadvantaged social backgrounds, with SEND, or newly arrived in the UK face difficulties accessing the school curriculum because of weaknesses in literacy skills or a variety of language difficulties or challenges. The ability to read and write effectively, as well as to communicate orally, are fundamental to both pupils' academic success and their well-being in school. Frustration caused by difficulties in understanding the particular language requirements of different subjects can lead to disaffection with school, poor social skills and low self-esteem. Poor literacy skills are common amongst pupils permanently excluded from school and in offenders in the prison system.

This chapter explores some of the links between disadvantage, low literacy levels and school achievement and well-being. It considers the strong link between low skills in literacy with patterns of school exclusion and offending. The chapter looks at some of the research from second language acquisition and research on the cultural reception and understanding of language of children from migrant and refugee backgrounds. It also draws on research on literacy across the curriculum initiatives that aim to help disadvantaged students.

Social disadvantage and language and literacy difficulties

As seen in Chapter 1, social disadvantage can have damaging consequences for the cognitive, emotional and social development of children. Studies from early years settings (eg Sylva et al., 2004) show that differences in literacy levels, particularly in speech and communication, surface very early in pre-school and infant school settings. McCoy (2013), in a study for the National Literacy Trust, estimates that one in six adults in the UK struggle with low literacy levels below those expected for an 11-year-old. These adults are less likely to be in full-time employment at the age of 30, and 63 per cent of men and 75 per cent of women with very low literacy skills have never achieved a work promotion.

Research (eg Kiernan and Mensah, 2011) has also consistently shown that children with parents with low incomes tend to have worse cognitive, academic and behavioural outcomes and are more likely to experience mental health problems (eg McLeod and Shanahan, 1993). Kiernan and Mensah also point out that positive parenting can make a difference for children despite poverty or family disadvantage. However, the material effects of poverty mean that children living in poor households often have less access to books, libraries and adult time for reading aloud when they are developing their language skills. This is not to blame parents but merely to point out that the pressures of poverty often mean that children in these circumstances often arrive in school with less developed language skills than many of their peers. They may also be tired and hungry.

Literacy, SEN and school exclusions

The research evidence that links literacy difficulties to both permanent and fixed-term school exclusion is also strong (eg Osler, Watling and Busher, 2001; Parkes, 2012; Slee, 2011). These studies suggest that many learners, who start with difficulties in the classroom, move through low self-esteem, poor behaviour and school exclusion to end up offending and in prison. In a discussion document published by the National Literacy Trust, Clark and Dugdale (2008) report that 70 per cent of pupils permanently excluded from school have difficulties in basic literacy skills. Macrae, McGuire and Milbourne (2008) argue that cultures of performativity mean young people with literacy and behavioural difficulties are particularly vulnerable to exclusion.

It is also well documented that there are huge social and financial costs as a result of literacy difficulties, as well as profound consequences for life prospects in adulthood (eg Bynner and Parsons, 1997). Over a quarter of children in the youth justice system have a learning disability, while more than three-quarters have serious difficulties with literacy (Newman et al., 2012). There are also significant differences in health-related practices and mental health between those with poor basic literacy and numeracy skills and those with good basic skills (Bynner and Parsons, 1997).

Literacy and permanent and fixed-term school exclusions

Permanent and fixed-term school exclusions have risen sharply in the UK in the last few years, and in England in particular, which has a much higher rate than the rest of the UK. The latest figures for 2015–16 for England show that there were 6685 permanent exclusions (up from 5795 in 2014–15 and 4630 in 2012–13). This corresponds to 35.2 permanent exclusions a day.

The characteristics of those young people excluded show that:

> » *pupils eligible for and claiming free school meals (FSM) were four times more likely to receive a permanent or fixed term exclusion than their peers;*
>
> » *pupils with identified SEN accounted for almost half of all permanent or fixed term exclusions;*
>
> » *pupils with SEN support had the highest permanent exclusion rate and were almost seven times more likely to receive a permanent exclusion than pupils with no SEN;*
>
> » *pupils with an Education, Health and Care (EHC) plan or with a statement of SEN had the highest fixed term exclusion rate and were almost six times more likely to receive a fixed term exclusion than pupils with no SEN;*
>
> » *pupils of Gypsy/Roma and Traveller of Irish Heritage ethnic groups had the highest rate of both permanent and fixed term exclusions (although as a relatively small population these figures should be treated with some caution);*
>
> » *black Caribbean pupils were over three times more likely to be permanently excluded than the school population as a whole.*

(DfE, 2017, p 5)

These figures suggest a strong link between social disadvantage and school exclusion for children living in poverty, with SEN and from particular ethnic minorities. Institutionalised racism and racist assumptions on the part of some educators are often cited as key factors for the very high rate of permanent exclusions for black Caribbean boys (eg Gillborn, 2008) It should also be pointed out that boys were three times more likely to be excluded than girls and that nearly half of all permanently excluded school pupils (48 per cent) were aged either 13 or 14.This age is not only the most volatile period of adolescence but also corresponds to the school years where, in the UK, the curriculum moves towards GCSE-style teaching and content.

Pupils with SEN are not only more likely to experience low academic achievement; they are also around seven or eight times more likely to be permanently excluded than those pupils with no SEN (Clark and Dugdale, 2008). Some research also points to the way in which factors may be interlinked; for example, Law and Sivyer (2003) argue that pupils with emotional and behavioural difficulties, which make them vulnerable to school exclusion, tend to have literacy and communication problems as well.

Literacy, exclusion and youth offending

There is clear research evidence that for many pupils educational failure in literacy is both strongly associated with the process of school exclusion and subsequent patterns of youth and adult offending. Research by Dyslexia Action (Rack, 2005) demonstrated that there is an over-representation within the prison population of those with literacy difficulties and those who have dyslexia or other language-specific learning difficulties (SpLD). At the time of this research:

» around 50% of the prison population were found to have poor literacy skills;

» 20% of offenders were found to be dyslexic, which is 10% above the population norm;

» 25% of young offenders were said to have reading skills below those of the average seven-year-old.

These findings built on existing results from a prison service study, which asks prisoners as they are admitted to take a literacy test devised by the Basic Skills Agency. The test was approximately equivalent to the reading skills expected of nine- to ten-year-olds. The 1998 results showed that 60 per cent had problems with literacy, and 40 per cent had severe literacy problems. Similarly, the Social Exclusion Unit (2002) reported that 80 per cent of prisoners had writing skills at or below the level expected of an 11-year-old child; the equivalent figure for reading was 50 per cent (Social Exclusion Unit: 6). There is a statistically significant connection between repeated offending and poor basic skills (Parsons, 2002).

According to Newman et al. (2012), over a quarter of children in the youth justice system have a learning disability, while more than three-quarters have serious difficulties with literacy. In a study by Hewitt-Main (2012), 53 per cent (2029) of prisoners at Chelmsford were diagnosed as having dyslexia, compared to 10 per cent of the UK population. This evidence, and that of other studies, suggests that many learners who start with difficulties in the classroom move through low self-esteem, poor behaviour and school exclusion to end up offending and in prison. In a study of 58 juvenile offenders aged 15–17, Bryan, Freer and Furlong (2007) found that 90 per cent of juvenile offenders in the sample had below average language skills with 46–67 per cent of these being in the poor or very poor group. Snowling et al. (2000) found significant levels of specific reading difficulties, including dyslexia, in young offenders. Bryan (2004) and Bryan, Freer and Furlong (2007) point to the prevalence of speech, language and communication difficulties in juvenile offenders.

Reading, writing and language impairment

Poor literacy skills can have both immediate and lasting consequences for young people. The Bercow Report (DfCSF, 2008) suggested that children with speech, language and communication needs are often frustrated at school and therefore are at significant risk of educational failure and school exclusion There is also strong evidence that having poor basic skills impacts adult outcomes, especially for individuals at high risk of social exclusion from other factors (Parsons and Bynner, 2002). Education, and the outcomes measured by educational attainment in the form of qualifications and test scores during compulsory schooling, is the most frequent and most effective predictor of adult outcomes, and of social exclusion (Sparkes and Glennerster, 2002). At age 16, over half of boys with poor reading skills think school is a waste of time and nearly four in five want to leave school as soon as possible. For these young people literacy problems are a key factor in disaffection from school.

Poor reading and other literacy skills are predictive of adult social exclusion; additional risk factors in childhood include social class, parents' education and living in overcrowded housing. An additional risk factor is having parents:

» with little understanding of their child's education;

» who are unsure about the value of education or training post-16; or

» who do not want their child to pursue further studies for financial reasons.

Carlile (2012) cites institutionalised racism as a factor in the lack of adequate translation facilities for the English language, which creates social boundaries between people and undermines the participation of parents in school exclusion and inclusion processes.

There is some evidence to suggest that behaviour problems and resulting school exclusions are associated with language impairment. Clegg et al. (2009) contend that for a high proportion of secondary-age pupils at risk of permanent school exclusion, language difficulties are a significant factor in their behavioural problems at school. In older children who are permanently excluded, expressive rather than receptive language impairment is more common and this is associated with increased levels of emotional problems (Ripley and Yuill, 2005).

Writing difficulties are commonly cited as key indicators of pupils struggling to meet the demands of the curriculum. Cremin and Myhill (2011) argue that it is the complex and recursive nature of writing that makes it difficult and problematic for many young writers, leading to disaffection with schooling. For example, in a study of permanent school exclusion (Daniels et al. 2003), many of the excluded young people interviewed reported a particular dislike for formal writing in school. Recent research on young and adolescent pupils experiencing difficulties with writing suggests that attention needs to be paid to the forms of social interaction played by active agents of change within mediated activity in the classroom (e.g. Fisher, 2011; Thompson and Wittek, 2016).

The costs of exclusion versus early prevention or literacy intervention

Poor literacy skills for the minority and consequent school exclusions are enormously damaging for society both at the time of the exclusion and in the long term. Research (eg Rack, 2005) suggests that the cost of supporting children with SEND who are excluded is in the region of £50 million per year. Brookes, Goodall and Heady (2007, p 1) estimated that:

» *the average cost to society of an excluded child was £63,851;*

» *the average cost of a persistent truant was £44,468 (split roughly between cost to the individual and the rest of society);*

» *this represents a total cost of £800 million per year.*

These alarming figures of course are much higher today. This funding would have been better used to provide appropriate early support in school as happens in other nations that are more successful in Programme for International Student Assessment (PISA) rankings. In Finland, for example, special needs intervention tends to happen in the early years and there are far fewer costs to society of SEN at secondary school level. Perhaps even more importantly, intervention is seen as something positive for the child.

A long-term study (Schweinhart, 2003) of the High/Scope Perry Pre-school Programme in an impoverished Michigan community in the USA provides evidence that quality pre-school education can exert a lasting, positive influence over children's lives through improving their social and communicative skills. This in turn helped to improve these children's receptiveness to literary acquisition. It calculated that for every $1 originally invested in the Perry Pre-school Programme, there has been a return to the taxpayer in reduced crime, lower demand for special education, welfare and other public services of over $7 in real terms. Similar results for early intervention have been reported in Finland (eg Sabel et al., 2010). Visser (2005) points out that that prevention is better than intervention for young people with SEND and argues that appropriate challenge is important for engagement.

In a study in the USA, Miles and Stipek (2006) investigated the associations between social skills (aggression and prosocial behaviour) and literacy achievement in a sample of four- to six-year-old elementary school children from low-family-income backgrounds. The results showed consistent association between good social skills and literacy achievement, although whilst the strength of the association between aggression and literacy achievement increased over the elementary grades the link between prosocial behaviour and literacy achievement decreased. Another of their key findings was that poor literacy achievement in the first and third grades (equivalent to Years 2 and 4 in the UK) predicted relatively high-aggressive behaviour in the third and fifth grades (Years 4 and 6 in the UK), respectively.

Macrae, McGuire and Milbourne (2003) point out that exclusion from primary school is particularly problematic, as it is at this time most children learn the basics of reading, writing and social interaction. Education and social interaction disrupted at this stage can be difficult to compensate for in later schooling (Hayden, 1996). Children excluded from primary school:

are an especially vulnerable minority. In England in 2015–16 1145 primary school pupils were permanently excluded, 290 of whom were aged six or younger. The pupils usually have some level of special educational need as well as disrupted and stressful family backgrounds. Their behaviour illustrates distress rather than 'naughtiness'.

(Hayden, 1996, p 235)

Parsons (2005) notes that the policy responses to exclusion emerge from national and local government decision-making and correlate with decisions in the criminal justice system about whether to resource prevention or punishment. Literacy difficulties are a social problem, not an individual or family deficit that should be punished. As seen in Chapter 2, literacy or other learning difficulties are not necessarily a permanent barrier to pupils' development or behaviour in school and, in the right circumstances, interventions can make a significant difference to the lives of disadvantaged young people. Education can mediate the effects of social disadvantage (eg Machin, 2006) and schools with collaborative cultures can make the biggest difference (eg Ortega, Thompson and Daniels, 2017).

English as an additional language

Modern classrooms in the UK are often increasingly multicultural and multilingual. This rich social and cultural diversity poses both pedagogical opportunities and challenges for teachers in schools and for teacher educators in preparing their trainee teachers in a variety of schools to teach their subject to students for whom English is an additional language (EAL). Despite the growing importance of EAL in UK schools, there is surprisingly little research on the effects of EAL on learning, and reading and writing skills in particular (eg Murphy, Kyriacou and Menon, 2015).

The British Council (2017) estimates that there are currently over a million EAL learners in UK-maintained schools and these numbers have continued to grow year on year. Figures show that:

> » *nearly 19% of the primary population of England has EAL and over 14% of the secondary population;*
> » *the numbers are lower in Scotland, Wales and Northern Ireland, but have grown rapidly in the last ten years;*
> » *in 2013 there were 29,000 EAL learners in Scottish schools;*
> » *in Wales in 2013 42,000 pupils were eligible for support from the Minority Ethnic Achievement Grant (MEAG);*
> » *Northern Ireland now has over 10,000 'Newcomer' pupils in its schools.*

(British Council, 2017)

Of course there is a huge diversity of EAL learners, and the government definition of an EAL learner includes '*all pupils who use or have access to more than one language at home or at school – it does not necessarily imply full fluency in both or all languages*' (DfES, 2003, p 2). EAL learners who arrive in the UK from overseas come from a huge range of different countries with experience of very different education systems and cultural backgrounds. Indeed, even children from the same country may have very diverse cultural, ethnic, religious, political or social class backgrounds. What these children have in common is that they use one or more language other than English at home or in their community. In many cases, EAL is a positive attribute for those children who speak two or more languages fluently. Indeed, evidence (eg Strand, 2014) shows that in the UK children from Chinese and Indian backgrounds overall do best in GCSE examinations. It can reasonably be assumed that many of these young people grew up to be bilingual or multilingual.

Nevertheless, although the academic achievement of children with EAL varies widely, there is a general trend for children with EAL not to match the educational achievement of monolingual English-speaking peers (Murphy, Kyriacou and Menon, 2015). For example, evidence from the Early Years Foundation Stage Profile, a wide-ranging assessment of children's physical, intellectual, emotional and social development, showed that in 2010–11 52 per cent of children who speak EAL achieved the expected 'good level of development' in comparison to 60 per cent of their English as a first language peers. EAL children lag behind their native-speaking peers on measures of reading comprehension and writing skill. The acquisition and use of English vocabulary, both expressive and academic, is a major factor in the academic and social success of EAL learners. In addition, for those children who come from extreme disadvantaged backgrounds, such as pupils from asylum-seeking or refugee backgrounds, acquiring EAL can constitute a considerable barrier to learning. Learning to communicate in a new language is a social process, and emotional problems can hamper social integration in school.

Children who are newly arrived immigrants to the UK (first generation) and children who were born in the UK but who did not speak English as their first language (second generation) are usually described as 'language minority children'. For both groups of language minority children, the first point of significant exposure to both social and academic English is during primary school years. The language of instruction in English schools is English, with no statutory right to be educated in another language.

Language-minority children educated through the medium of the majority language face multiple challenges at school:

» developing a level of English language proficiency required for academic purposes;

» integrating socially into new peer groups;

» acquiring new academic skills and knowledge;

» distinguishing between different registers in social and academic spoken English;

» developing reading and writing skills in English;

» understanding cultural differences.

As González, Moll and Amanti (2005) have demonstrated, success here depends on the EAL learners' ability to acquire language skills required of the academic tasks and their ability to bridge the cultural and socio-economic differences between home and school. This means schools valuing the 'funds of knowledge' that children bring with them from the first language as well as their social and cultural backgrounds. For the most part, EAL children are taught in mainstream classes in the UK and not withdrawn for any significant period of time due to limited English proficiency. Good practice also suggests that newly arrived EAL learners should not be placed in lower ability sets. Designated EAL coordinators and teachers are available in some schools to help provide support to EAL pupils, but in many cases EAL comes under the jurisdiction of SENCOs. This sends the wrong message that EAL is akin to a learning difficulty. Of course some EAL pupils do have SEND, but the blanket association of EAL with learning difficulties can have very harmful consequences. In practice, EAL teachers are relatively rare, even in schools with high numbers of EAL pupils.

Although generalising about EAL learners can be problematic, it is fair to say that they may:

» have gaps in understanding of academic vocabulary and conventions of written language;

» have less grasp of idiomatic speech as their understanding tends to be literal;

» display a disparity between confidence in their social and academic talk;

» struggle with language and grammatical features such as verb tense forms, pronouns, connectives, subject–verb agreement, word order, prepositions and determiners.

However, EAL learners can also bring positive attributes to learning such as: commitment and purpose; an understanding that languages and grammars differ; and written and oral knowledge of their first language(s). Well-resourced schools can draw from the first-language knowledge of the pupils where possible, particularly if teachers or support staff have knowledge of that language. Common weaknesses in EAL provision include:

» a lack of specialised staff;

» a lack of provision for more advanced bilingual learners (not newly arrived);

» management of EAL provision being an ill-defined role, often carried out informally by a teaching assistant;

» a lack of clarity in distinctions between EAL and SEN.

Another critique is that whilst many schools show great sensitivity to issues of cultural diversity, the EAL practice shows little awareness of the language demands of the curriculum. Language development needs are often masked by competence in oral language (this can be true of first language learners as well). Research has shown that it is possible for newly arrived EAL pupils to develop Basic Interpersonal Communicative Skills (BICS) in conversational fluency in one year and conversational English within two to three years. It takes between five and seven years for EAL pupils to operate on a par with their monolingual peers. However, it may take longer to become proficient in using academic English, which is described as having Cognitive Academic Language Proficiency (CALP).

There is a need for both more EAL-focused training and EAL pedagogy in classrooms. For example, reading comprehension difficulties in EAL learners are often masked by strong phonological and word decoding skills. But simple decoding is not the same as reading for meaning. Comprehension of written language is critical to children's reading development, as children progress from 'learning to read' to 'reading to learn'. Reading comprehension also increases academic vocabulary and CALP. Much of the literature (eg Cummins, 2000) stresses the need for contextual support for pupils learning EAL. This includes:

» *making connections with and building on pupils' experience;*

» *creating space to use existing knowledge;*

» *giving opportunities to talk around a topic across the curriculum;*

» *encouraging the use of first language;*

» *building a framework for organising thinking, using key visuals;*

» *using visual clues;*

» *providing concrete examples of impersonal and abstract concepts.*

(Milton Keynes EMASS, 2006, p 8)

In addition to encouraging EAL pupils to use language in meaningful ways, teachers should help them to understand that learning a new language involves learning new words, idioms, accents and dialects and that errors are a normal part of the learning process (eg Brown, 2007). A supportive school learning environment is also important based on:

» structured lessons that draw pupils in from the start of the lesson;

» active and engaging tasks which encourage all pupils to participate;

» teaching and learning strategies that are oral and interactive;

» an emphasis on short-term planning, which includes planning for input and support from other adults in the classroom, to ensure the learning opportunities are maximised;

» subject-specific language skills and the teaching of conventions of particular forms of writing, which are made explicit and demonstrated by the teacher;

» planned opportunities for oral rehearsal in pairs and in small groups;

» a requirement that pupils apply learning, supported by group work, before moving to independent activity.

(Adapted from Milton Keynes EMASS, 2006)

These strategies are beneficial for both EAL and first-language learners and share a conception of learning as a social activity that leads to development (Bruner, 1960; Vygotsky, 1987).

Language and literacy across the curriculum

Since the 1975 Bullock Report *Language for Life*, there has been widespread acceptance that literacy is both a key to pupils' learning and a whole school issue. Yet one of the conclusions of the All-Party Parliamentary Group for Education's *Report of the Inquiry into Overcoming the Barriers to Literacy* in 2011 was that secondary schools *'should be developing cross-departmental strategies to improve literacy, rather than working in departmental silos'* (p 3). In the same report, whilst secondary teachers were seen as more likely than primary school teachers to express concerns about low literacy levels of pupils they were less likely to see this as a whole school problem.

Literacy Across the Curriculum (LAC) is a renewed focus for Ofsted inspections of both primary and secondary schools. The former Head of Ofsted, Michael Wilshaw, criticised secondary schools in particular for lacking effective programmes for developing literacy skills across the curriculum. In fact, many UK secondary schools' curriculums have long incorporated some attention to language in learning and to literacy across the curriculum, although this has varied considerably from institution to institution. In a recent, as yet unpublished, research project funded by the Oxford University Press, I have found a strong correlation between active and consistent secondary school LAC policies and progress in English and literacy skills. Effective policies improve reading, writing, and speaking and listening skills through work in particular subject disciplines that makes effective cross-curricular links with other subjects. Teachers in these schools also have a strong understanding of written conventions for writing genres appropriate to their subject and the ways that these genres may be used in other subjects. So, for example, an English teacher might ask pupils to write a recipe for a Shakespearean tragedy and a science teacher might ask pupils to use narrative report.

The revised national curriculum for English (2014) places a high importance on the teaching and learning of spoken language, reading, writing and vocabulary in pupils' cognitive, social and linguistic development across the whole curriculum:

Teachers should develop pupils' spoken language, reading, writing and vocabulary as integral aspects of the teaching of every subject. English is both a subject in its own right and the medium for teaching; for pupils, understanding the language provides access to the whole curriculum. Fluency in the English language is an essential foundation for success in all subjects.

(DfE, 2013, p 10)

In a critique of the revised national curriculum for English, the National Association of Teachers of English (NATE) argued that the government mistakenly prioritises pre-competence analytical learning in the younger years (NATE, 2016).They make the point that competence comes prior to analysis and that it is therefore wrong to expect all learners to leave primary school as the equivalent of adult reader, writers and speakers. NATE further suggests that the government's insistence on the primacy of the method of systematic synthetic phonics in primary school teaching of reading is also wrong. This reliance on decoding through phonological awareness does not do '*justice to the hypothesis-forming, rule-testing, rule-adapting, memory-employing, meaning-making complex activity which is reading*' (NATE, 2016, p 4). Of course grapho-phonic knowledge can help children understand some English words, but many words in English, including some of the most common, do not follow the rules of grapho-phonic correspondence. Teaching a range of reading strategies, and fostering an enjoyment of reading, are far more important.

At secondary school level, an Ofsted study shows that in schools with effective LAC policies leaders and managers at all levels appreciated that there was a range of effective strategies and that departments might identify different literacy priorities and approaches as being particularly useful in their subject area. These schools challenged pupils to engage challenging concepts, make connections between subjects and learn from others. The key features of schools with effective LAC policies were that:

» *long-term planning for literacy, rather than a focus on 'quick fixes', is understood to be important;*

» *head teachers and senior leaders give active, consistent and sustained support;*

» *the need is recognised to make the case for literacy in all subjects and answer the question for teachers, 'What's in it for us?';*

» *effective use is made of specialist knowledge to support individual departments and teachers;*

» *teachers are encouraged to identify effective practice in different areas of the curriculum and to learn from each other;*

» *there is an emphasis on practical ideas that teachers can use in longer term plans and schemes of work;*

» *effective use is made of the library and librarian;*

» *senior leaders keep a close eye on developments through systematic monitoring and evaluation.*

(Ofsted, 2013, pp 5–6)

Teachers as writers

It has long been acknowledged that pupils can learn from experienced adult writers about the discipline of writing and redrafting. However, Cremin and Oliver (2017), in a systematic review, highlight the importance of teachers being conscious of themselves as writers as a way of engaging pupils as writers.

Most teachers of literacy in primary school have entered teaching through a generalist route. The Teachers as Writers (TAW) project set out to pair primary school literacy teachers with professional writers so that they could share in a community of writers. The findings from the project suggested that this engagement was valuable for the confidence of these teachers and this enhanced their ability to teach writing to their pupils. Pedagogic changes were made as a result of strengthened writer identities. The TAW project made the following recommendations that teachers working with school pupils as writers should:

» *offer time and space for pupil freewriting sessions;*

» *write alongside pupils, acting as role-models;*

» *pay attention to pupils' writing identities;*

» *make richer use of feedback and peer-editing to support revision;*

» *explore the personal dimension of writing, alongside the social and emotional demands involved.*

(Teachers as Writers, 2017, p 8)

IN A **NUTSHELL**

There is a proven link between poverty and social disadvantage and low levels of literacy. Being a poor reader, writer or communicator can lead to disruptive behaviour in school. Many young people with literacy difficulties, also have emotional behavioural difficulties, putting them at risk of disengagement from schooling, permanent exclusion and poor future life prospects. Low literacy levels have enormous social and financial costs to individuals, families and society as a whole. The UK also has growing numbers of EAL learners with a wide range of linguistic needs. However, effective literacy and EAL teaching, LAC policies and positive school culture can reverse the relationship between poor literacy skills, school attainment and disruptive school behaviour.

REFLECTIONS ON **CRITICAL ISSUES**

- *There is a strong relationship between social disadvantage and language and literacy difficulties for many young people.*

- *There is also a strong link between language and literacy difficulties and exclusion from school.*

- *There are both short- and long-term negative consequences of poor language and literacy skills.*

- *English as an Additional Language pupils have a wide variety of needs but these are most acute when linked to social disadvantage.*

- *Effective language across the curriculum policies and practice can help disadvantaged pupils.*

CHAPTER 5 | RESEARCHING POVERTY AND TEACHER EDUCATION

> ### CRITICAL **ISSUES**
>
> - What is the relationship between educational research and educational policy?
>
> - What constitutes effective evidence in educational research?
>
> - What are some of the potential uses and misuses of practitioner research?
>
> - How do schools increase research literacy?
>
> - How can schools and universities research together?
>
> - What forms of research can make a difference in removing barriers to learning caused by social disadvantage?

Introduction

The final chapter focuses on the potential for future educational research designs on the effects of social disadvantage on young people in schools and the debates about what constitutes research evidence. The chapter discusses some potential uses and misuses of practitioner research, including action research, and its relationship with academic research. It argues that whilst some researchers have created a false dichotomy between academic and practitioner research, there is still a need for more research literacy within schools and engagement with schools and teachers from academics in educational research. This is particularly true of research regarding social disadvantage in education. In order to illustrate these arguments, the chapter draws on some of the lessons from findings of research conducted by the author and others on: secondary schools' use of the pupil premium; the large-scale randomised control trial study *Closing the Gap: Test and Learn*; and interventionist research projects.

The relationship between educational research and educational policy

There has been significant investment and targeted intervention to try to narrow the gap in attainment by successive governments in the past decade. However, a recent report from the Education Policy Institute suggests that:

> » *the gap between disadvantaged children and their peers has narrowed only marginally by three months of learning between 2007–2016;*
>
> » *based on current trends it will take 50 years before there is an equitable education system where the disadvantaged do not fall behind;*
>
> » *for those considered 'persistently disadvantaged', entitled to free school meals for 80% of their time at secondary school, the gap has widened to an average of over two years of learning by the end of secondary school;*
>
> » *the divide continues to emerge in the early years and increase throughout education.*

(Andrews, Robinson and Hutchinson, 2017, p 6)

Of course, 'closing the gap' in itself does not mean eradicating poverty or other forms of disadvantage. Even the best-quality education cannot entirely solve deep-rooted social and economic inequality. Nevertheless, the challenge for policy makers, for educational researchers and for teachers in schools to address disadvantage remains an ethical and social imperative. However, Hammersley (2002) has made the point that the relationship between educational research, policy making and educational practice in schools has long been a fraught one. Attempts to address this relationship have lurched from crisis to crisis with educational research situated in universities periodically derided or dismissed by politicians as being irrelevant to the practices of schools. These periodic crises have tended to distort any real discussion of:

> » *the roles that educational research has* actually *played;*
>
> » *the roles that educational research* can *play;*
>
> » *the roles that educational research* ought *to play.*

(Hammersley, 2002, p 1)

There are also questions of how educational research is interpreted. Some of the most rigorous educational research has shown that excellent teaching is the biggest influence on learning and achievement and improving teacher quality the most effective investment (eg Hattie, 2003). Improving the quality of teaching has the greatest effect on pupils' achievement (Sammons et al., 2014). Hattie has shown that the majority of the first ten factors which influence learning are in the hands of the teacher:

Influence	Effect size	Source of influence
Feedback	1.13	Teacher
Students' prior cognitive ability	1.04	Student
Instructional quality	1.00	Teacher
Direct instruction	0.82	Teacher

Influence	Effect size	Source of influence
Remediation/feedback	0.65	Teacher
Students' disposition to learn	0.61	Student
Class environment	0.56	Teacher
Challenge of goals	0.52	Teacher
Peer tutoring	0.50	Teacher
Mastery learning	0.50	Teacher

(Hattie, 2003, p 4)

This very strong evidence, taken from a review of the literature and a synthesis of over a half a million studies, suggests that expert teachers make a difference to pupils' learning. The obvious implication is that policy initiatives should be aimed at creating and nurturing expert teachers and helping other teachers to become expert. However, the teaching profession in the UK from my own experience as a teacher and teacher educator has recently felt under siege. Performance targets, rising class sizes and seemingly constant curriculum changes have driven many expert teachers out of the classroom. Similarly, research that 'setting' has negative consequences for disadvantaged students has been largely ignored by policy makers.

Closing the gap?

There is also the question of who should do educational research. Teacher research literacy and evidence-based practice for teaching and learning have been high priorities for recent governments both in England and in the rest of the UK. In England, Teaching Schools have research as part of their remit and the National College for Teaching and Leadership has supported high-profile research initiatives such as Closing the Gap: Test and Learn. Teacher research conferences have been well attended and popular with many in the profession. Educational research has recently been challenged to produce rigorous evidence that can guide teaching practice.

The question, of course, is what constitutes rigorous evidence. Under the Coalition government, it was clear that quantitative studies, and in particular randomised controlled trials (RCTs), became the preferred method for educational research. The clearest manifestation of these was Michael Gove's commissioning of a report by the medical journalist and researcher Ben Goldacre, which argued for medical-style RCTs in education. Menter and Thompson (in press) have argued that whilst there is clearly an important place for RCTs, an over-reliance on this method can ignore important questions of social and cultural context. RCTs may be able to tell us whether one approach works better in terms of effect than others, but they cannot on their own tell us why. Another danger is that favouring RCTs above other methods can devalue both qualitative research and practitioner research.

The National College for Teaching and Leadership (NCTL)-led project *Closing the Gap: Test and Learn* is an interesting example of both the strengths and limitations of large-scale evidence-based research. The NCTL worked with key universities and research organisations to develop the project and involved teaching schools and their alliances in the research. The project found that very few of the interventions evaluated made a significant difference to disadvantaged learners' progress. At the same time, the project involved hundreds of schools and several hundred teachers who became more research literate through involvement in the project. Some schools even developed their own small-scale quasi-experimental research. In this way, the NCTL project helped to expand research capacity in England.

Another example was the establishment of the Education Endowment Foundation (EEF). The EEF was set up with a strong remit to supporting and testing projects that help disadvantaged pupils. RCTs were cited as an appropriate method for these evaluations as they can be replicated and scaled up. The EEF has also used systematic reviews in order to synthesise existing research. The subsequent Teaching and Learning Toolkits have been valuable resources to schools, although Wiliam (*TES*, 2015) and others have warned that systematic reviews in education can miss questions of context and variables. The point about research literacy is that schools and teachers need to be able to review research evidence in relation to the contexts that they work in.

As seen throughout this book, the relationship between poverty and education is both evident and very complex. This means there is a need for both complex policy and interventions that make a difference. Raffo et al. (2007, p 1), in a review of the research evidence, make the following conclusions.

> » *The research indicates a corresponding need for extensive and complex policy interventions if the established relationship between poverty and poor educational outcomes is to be disturbed. There are no specific problems which can be fixed by either a 'magic bullet' or 'scatter gun' approach.*

> » *The researchers conclude that breaking the link between education and poverty demands a change in underlying structures and power relations and a coherent set of integrated and multi-level interventions. The issues facing policy makers are:*

> – *how to make multiple interventions coherent;*

> – *how to sequence them chronologically;*

> – *that skills and knowledge can be transferred across different contexts of learning; and*

> – *how to prioritise the most effective or most important.*

(Raffo et al., 2007)

Teachers as researchers

Practitioner research, either as part of an accredited higher education course or as professional development, is a key and growing part of many teachers' practice.

Ironically, it was two of the educational researchers most well known to teachers in UK schools who offered a critique of the view that teachers should be increasingly involved in educational research. Dylan Wiliam's editorial for the *Times Educational Supplement* (*TES*) was titled 'The Research Delusion' (*TES*, April 2015). Behind the inflammatory headline lies a more nuanced and thoughtful argument. In the article Wiliam explained that whilst the desire to make teaching a research-led profession was well-intentioned it was not in his opinion possible, not least because of the difficulty schools might find in locating and interpreting research evidence. Similarly, John Hattie, in an interview two weeks after Wiliam's article appeared, was reported to have said:

Researching is a particular skill. Some of us took years to gain that skill. Asking teachers to be researchers? They are not. I want to put the emphasis on teachers as evaluators of their impact. Be skilled at that. Whereas the whole research side, leave that to the academics.

(TES, April 2015)

Of course Hattie has a point here, and large-scale research evaluations and interventions do need both research expertise and lots of resources. However, there are dangers in separating the teaching profession's concerns with research evidence and those of professional educational researchers. In particular, such a separation can create a false dichotomy, which suggests that:

> » on the one hand, professional practice research: is done by teachers and schools; is necessarily small scale; and aims to improve existing practice for a particular teacher or school;

> » on the other hand, academic research: is done to teachers and schools; is large scale; aims to research teaching and learning in schools by examining existing practice or by testing interventions; and aims to have impact by informing policy.

These descriptions oversimplify the situation of course and many research projects involve partnerships between schools and universities often linked to ITE programmes or masters and doctoral programmes.

Research partnerships

One example of a research partnership is the ITE clinical practice model of the Oxford Internship (see Hagger and McIntyre, 2006). The Oxford Internship scheme was set up by the Department of Education at the University of Oxford in collaborative partnership with the Oxfordshire Local Education Authority and its local secondary schools. The commitment to school-based and research-led teacher training was underpinned by '*sustained critical dialogue between the different kinds of expertise which teachers and university lecturers could bring as equal partners to considerations of teaching expertise*' (Hagger and McIntyre, 2006, p 15). The educational landscape may have changed, particularly in school governance and the role of local educational authorities, but the collaborative partnership between the university and Oxfordshire schools under the recently formed Oxford Education Deanery remains strong in both ITE and in educational research (Fancourt, Edwards and Menter, 2015). The ITE clinical practice approach stresses both the dialectical interplay between theories of education and teaching practice as well as the developmental importance of disrupting and questioning previous assumptions about pedagogy and the ways particular people learn in particular circumstances. This is done through the concept of practical theorising (Hagger and McIntyre, 2006), which involves subjecting theory to critical examination in the light of experience in classrooms.

Practitioner and action research

Practitioner research often involves teachers reviewing and reflecting on their own teaching practice in particular social situations. Practitioner research in education in some senses picked up the concerns of Dewey regarding the validity of educational research:

The answer is that (1) educational practices provide the data, the subject-matter, which form the problems of inquiry... These educational practices are also (2) the final test of value of the conclusions of all researches... Actual activities in education test the worth of scientific results... They may be scientific in some other field, but not in education until they serve educational purposes, and whether they really serve or not can be found out only in practice.

(Dewey, 1929, p 33)

The criticism of much practitioner research is that it is often both small scale, context bound and not generalisable. It could also be argued that this form of research is highly subjective. The danger here is that an over-focus on the self as an actor means that aspects of practices, processes or aspects can be overlooked. Reflexivity in relation to inquiry into phenomena is central to the critical-analytical tradition. In this sense of reflexive research, informing and transforming practice, the best-practitioner research involves a critical-analytical methodology that acknowledges the role of the researcher as a participant.

The term 'action research' is generally credited to Kurt Lewin who was concerned with research that leads to social action (Lewin, 1948). Concerns of power, justice and social improvement underpin almost all advocates of action research in the field of education. Lewin's methodology involves data collection and evaluation based on an initial or general idea, which then follows cycles of planning, action and evaluation of the result of action. Criticism of the approach outlined in Lewin's model argues that this form of action research is flawed because the general idea may be fixed in advance and research may become merely an attempt to find facts to validate the initial theory.

On the other hand, such a structured form of action research can be an important tool of teacher professional development designed to change practice. Discussions of action research focus both on the situated nature of educational activity and the wider contexts of practice. In effect, some versions of action research try to move from a micro-analysis of particular instances to a macro-analysis of wider social contexts. This process of moving from a micro-analysis of instances of classroom activity that provokes questions and categories for interpretive analysis, towards a macro-analysis of the implications for pedagogy, is integral to the best examples of practitioner research.

Perhaps above all, practitioner research in education is about challenging and changing practice in order to improve the educational experience of pupils. Practitioner research is often highly visible in schools and sometimes mediated through contact with academics or other practitioner researchers. Although much of this research will not be generalisable, reflecting on and changing practice can have important benefits for disadvantaged young people, particularly in schools with strong collaborative cultures.

Improved teacher research literacy can also mean increased sensitivity to the contexts of research, an understanding of analytic rigour and a thoughtful, critical stance to interpreting data.

Researching disadvantage in education

This chapter has stressed the importance of collaborative approaches to researching disadvantage in education. This final section looks at two very different research projects in order to illustrate the ways that university researchers and education professionals can engage in meaningful collaborative research.

Researching the pupil premium grant

This research project (Burn et al., 2016) used the introduction of the Pupil Premium Grant (PPG) for state-funded schools in England aimed at raising the attainment of disadvantaged pupils as a stimulus to explore trainee teachers' and school teachers' understandings of the effects of poverty on young people. The PPG is additional government funding to schools for disadvantaged pupils, where eligibility for free school meals in the last six years is the main measure of deprivation.

The intervention, jointly designed by colleagues at the university and its partnership schools, required all students to undertake a small-scale collaborative research project investigating the use of PPG funding within their second placement school in any way that they and the school's professional tutor (the teacher responsible for co-ordinating their school learning) chose. For example, some groups explored the impact of the PPG spending in school on the PPG pupils by exploring the stated aims of school interventions with the perceptions of the pupils affected. In most cases this involved direct contact with PPG students through interviews of focus groups. The research was to be presented to the senior management of the school who were responsible for justifying their expenditure to central government.

The mixed methods research design explored both the professional tutors' perspectives and choices about the project within their distinctive school settings as well as the beginning teachers' thoughts about their experiences within those particular contexts. The methods of data collection had been trialled the previous year when the project was implemented as a pilot study in a number of partnership schools. Detailed case studies were conducted within six partnership schools: three in large urban areas and three in predominantly rural areas. Each involved an interview with the professional tutor, observation of the beginning teachers' presentations in school and individual interviews with three of the beginning teachers.

Evaluation data across the whole partnership suggested that the projects operated successfully in most cases with the students encouraged to ask critical questions about current practices intended to support the learning of young people living in poverty, and to relate those practices to other sources of evidence. The questionnaire data indicated that over 90 per cent of respondents (n = 140) had the opportunity to carry out the PPG investigation in their second placement school. The majority (74 per cent) regarded it as a valuable learning experience that had enabled them to develop a better understanding of both the PPG and the government policy underpinning it, as well as of the ways in which their individual schools were using the funding and any difficulties associated with it. The final element of the research was a series of questions asked of all the beginning teachers involved in the research projects about their experience of the investigation and their perceptions of its value.

The case studies revealed considerable variation in the nature of the projects undertaken by the students and in their complex social situations of development. However, both the individual cases and the whole-course evaluation data suggest that the project was effectively implemented in the vast majority of schools, enabling the students to engage with issues of poverty and its relationship to young people's educational experiences and outcomes. Direct experience of talking to children in poverty and of evaluating PPG spending allowed them to better understand the constraints to learning experienced by these young people. However, some beginning teachers were critical of their schools' defensive reactions to the research and the fact that 10 per cent of the students were not given the opportunity to carry out an investigation hints at the range of constraints and challenges for this sort of research. There was also a wide variation in the attitudes of professional tutors to poverty. Whilst most were aware of the complexity of the relationship between learning and disadvantage, a minority appeared to hold deficit ideologies (see Chapter 3) that were not challenged by the PPG project.

A further consideration is the need to analyse the complex relationship between individual learning and the social situations of development in which that learning occurs. The research task was the deliberate introduction of a stimulus designed to mediate the experience for the beginning teachers of teaching disadvantaged students. In this form of practical theorising, the experience of research was mediated both through presenting the findings to other staff in the school and the subsequent discussion of the learning observed. This was so for both initial teachers in schools with high concentrations of disadvantaged students and those where the issue was largely hidden.

Creating a social situation of development around research helped in many cases to stimulate recontextualisation of knowledge about the effects of poverty for the beginning teachers. The practice-based meanings developed in understanding the use of the PPG through research was effective precisely because they were open to scrutiny, critique and recontextualisation through the process of practical theorising. The participants in the project were actively involved in the interpretation of the complexities of poverty and education rather than being told what to think by school or university mentors. These findings offer hope that creating social situations of development around disadvantage can encourage beginning teachers to learn to use, question and develop different kinds of evidence and different ways of thinking. Through this process of practical theorising they can develop new understandings of their role in making schooling more equitable for children living in poverty.

The research reported here also reaffirms the importance of designing interventions that take account of the different object motives that students encounter in school–university partnerships. Students are engaged in a multi-layered social situation of development within the specific social and cultural contexts of both their placement schools and their university environment (Tatto et al., forthcoming). The findings reported here suggest that if ITE programmes are to engage meaningfully with wider issues of social justice and reframe beginning teachers' thoughts about poverty and learning, then more attention needs to be paid within such programmes to the conflicting object motives of professional tutors, beginning teachers and mentors and to the mediating role of individual, social and institutional histories and experiences. The findings also confirm that in social situations of development of educational complexity, such as working with students living in poverty, contextualised intervention may be needed to disrupt previously held professional assumptions and positions.

Intervening outside the classroom

Adolescents who are struggling to develop both the empathy needed for collaboration and their own emotional needs, as well as the understanding of the criteria for academic success, can often experience periods of intense turbulence. Research also suggests that particular attention needs to be given to these children's subjective experience of well-being, their sense of purpose, meaning and engagement. Disadvantaged young people on the margins of society may lack the agency needed to negotiate schooling. Of course the concept of agency in the classroom context involves complex social, cultural and environmental factors including pupils' histories and present realities, teacher and pupil interaction, as well as pupil-to-pupil interaction. But what about those young people who have become socially excluded from school?

This study (Elliott and Dingwall, 2017; Thompson and Tawell, 2017), funded by Artswork, the South-east Bridge, focused on the effects of arts-based interventions for young people deemed at risk of school exclusion because of social, emotional and behavioural difficulties. The intervention took place outside the school settings in a professional theatre and in community spaces where these young people worked with professional artists and theatre practitioners. The research was designed in collaboration with the arts-based organisations who were eager to evaluate the effect of their work. Using a range of qualitative methods, including a series of observations of the arts sessions and interviews with the young people and arts professionals, the study explored the potential for creative arts interventions to transform young people's (aged 11–16) difficult social situations of development and, in so doing, effect changes in behaviour and way of being.

For many of the young people, the interventions were transformational. This was particularly true when the arts-based professionals also had effective pedagogical skills. The findings suggest that the interventions that the arts organisation offered these young people provided alternatives to their personal, cultural and historical ways of experiencing the world. In 'becoming other' as artists, experimenting with different art media, acting in role and trying out creative ideas within a safe environment, the young people chose to try out becoming a different version of themselves. This process of adopting a new identity in becoming an artist enabled some young people to recontextualise their relationship with the social worlds around them. The introduction of an element of socialised play through creative arts interventions helped these young people to negotiate the crisis of a social situation of development. The interventions gave the young people:

» respite from a difficult social situation;

» non-judgmental settings;

» resignification of learning and attitudes to adults/teachers;

» positive relationships;

» autonomy;

» resilience;

» and a set of emotional tools to cope with life.

These findings suggest that imagination, invoked through the social situation of play, can help some disengaged young people to change their perceptions about the imagined worlds of the future. Arts-based projects, led by practitioners skilled in both arts and pedagogy, enabled these young people to acquire tools for self-transformation.

IN A **NUTSHELL**

Tackling social disadvantage through educational research is a high priority for government, academic researchers and teachers in schools. However, the relationship between educational research and policy is a complex one that has led to mistrust and confusion as to what constitutes effective research. Practitioner and academic research has often been seen as existing in separate worlds rather than being complementary, but different, forms of research. Improved teacher research literacy can also mean increased sensitivity to the contexts of research, an understanding of analytic rigour, and a thoughtful, critical stance to interpreting data. Collaboration between schools and universities can lead to increased teacher research literacy and effective forms of research.

REFLECTIONS ON **CRITICAL ISSUES**

- *The relationship between educational research and educational policy is a complex one and has historically been characterised by a series of crises.*

- *Different forms of research can have validity in different contexts.*

- *Practitioner research is most effective when it is outward looking and focused on the learning needs of disadvantaged pupils.*

- *Practitioner research, engagement with academic research and participation in large-scale projects can all help improve teacher research literacy.*

- *Collaboration between schools and universities can produce effective research projects.*

- *Research has also shown that some particularly vulnerable pupils can benefit from arts-based interventions.*

REFERENCES

Andrews, J, Hutchinson, J and Johnes, R (2016) *Grammar Schools and Social Mobility*. London: Education Policy Institute.

Andrews, J, Robinson, D and Hutchinson, J (2017) *Closing the Gap? Trends in Educational Attainment and Disadvantage*. London: Education Policy Institute.

Ayers, W (1995) Popular Education: Teaching for Social Justice. *Democracy and Education*, 10(2): 5–8.

Ball, SJ (2003) *Class Strategies and the Education Market: The Middle Classes and Social Advantage*. London: Routledge.

Ball, SJ (2006) *Education Policy and Social Class: The Selected Works of Stephen J. Ball*. London: Routledge.

Ball, SJ (2016) Education, Justice and Democracy: The Struggle over Ignorance and Opportunity, in Montgomery, A and Kehoe, I (eds) *Reimagining the Purpose of Schools and Educational Organisations* (pp 189–205). Heidelberg: Springer.

Beckett, L (2016) *Teachers and Academic Partners in Urban Schools: Threats to Professional Practice*. Abingdon: Routledge.

BERA-RSA (2014) *Research and the Teaching Profession – Building Capacity for a Self-improving Education System*. London: BERA (available at bera.ac.uk).

Black, P and Wiliam, D (2005) A Theory for Assessment for Learning, in Gardner, J (ed) *Assessment and Learning* (pp 81–100). London: SAGE.

Bramley, G, Hirsch, D, Littlewood, M and Watkins, D (2016) *Counting the Cost of UK Poverty*. York: Joseph Rowntree Foundation.

British Council (2017) *EAL Learners in the UK*. Retrieved from: https://eal.britishcouncil.org/teachers/eal-learners-in-uk (accessed 15/09/17).

Brookes, M, Goodall, E, and Heady, L (2007) *Misspent Youth: The Costs of Truancy and Exclusion – A Guide for Donors and Funders*. London: New Philanthropy Capital.

Brown, HD (2007) *Teaching by Principles: An Interactive Approach to Language Pedagogy*. White Plains, NY: Pearson Education.

Bruner, J (1960) *The Process of Education*. Cambridge, MA: Harvard University Press.

Bryan, K (2004) Prevalence of Speech and Language Difficulties in Young Offenders. *International Journal of Language and Communication Disorders*, 39: 391–400.

Bryan, K, Freer, J and Furlong, C (2007) Language and Communication Difficulties in Juvenile Offenders. *International Journal of Language and Communication Disorders*, 42: 505–20.

Buras, KL (2014) There Really Is a Culture of Poverty: Notes on Black Working-class Struggles for Equity and Education, in Gorski, PC and Landsman, J (eds) *The Poverty and Education Reader: A Call for Equity in Many Voices* (pp 60–75). Herndon, VA: Stylus Publishing, LLC.

Burn, K and Childs, A (2016) Responding to Poverty through Education and Teacher Education Initiatives: A Critical Evaluation of Key Trends in Government Policy in England 1997–2015. *Journal of Education for Teaching*, 42(4): 387–403.

Burn, K, Hagger, K and Mutton, T (2015) *Beginning Teachers' Learning: Making Experience Count*. Northwich: Critical Publishing.

Burn, K, Mutton, T, Thompson, I, Ingram, J, McNicholl, J and Firth, R (2016) The Impact of Adopting a Research Orientation Towards Use of the Pupil Premium Grant in Preparing Beginning Teachers in England to Understand and Work Effectively with Young People Living in Poverty. *Journal of Education for Teaching*, 42(4): 434–450.

Burnett, B and Lampert, J (2015) Teacher Education for High-poverty Schools in Australia: The National Exceptional Teachers for Disadvantaged Schools Program, in Lampert, J and Burnett, B (eds) *Teacher Education for High Poverty Schools* (pp 73–94). New York: Springer Press.

Burns, S, Leitch, M and Hughes, J (2015) *Education Inequalities in Northern Ireland: Final Report to the Equality Commission for Northern Ireland*. Belfast: Queen's University.

Bynner, J and Parsons, S (1997) *It Doesn't Get Any Better: The Impact of Poor Basic Skills on the Lives of 37 Year Olds*. London: The Basic Skills Agency.

Bynner, J and Parsons, S (2002) Social Exclusion and the Transition from School to Work: The Case of Young People Not in Education, Employment, or Training (NEET). *Journal of Vocational Behavior*, 60(2): 289–309.

Carlile, A (2012) An Ethnography of Permanent Exclusion from School: Revealing and Untangling the Threads of Institutionalized Racism. *Race Ethnicity and Education*, 15(2): 175–94.

Carpenter, H, Papps, I, Bragg, J, Dyson, A, Harris, D, Kerr, K, Todd, L and Laing, K (2013) *Evaluation of Pupil Premium*. London: Department for Education.

Clark, C and Dugdale, G (2008) *Literacy Changes Lives: The Role of Literacy in Offending Behaviour*. London: The National Literacy Trust.

Claxton, G (2007) Expanding Young People's Capacity to Learn. *British Journal of Educational Studies*, 55(2): 115–34.

Clegg, J, Stackhouse, J, Finch, K, Murphy, C and Nicholls, S (2009) Language Abilities of Secondary Age Pupils at Risk of School Exclusion: A Preliminary Report. *Child Language Teaching and Therapy*, 25(1): 123–40.

Cochran-Smith, M (2004) *Walking the Road – Race, Diversity and Social Justice in Teacher Education*. New York: Teachers' College Press.

Cochran-Smith, M (2010) Towards a Theory of Teacher Education for Social Justice, in Fullan, M, Hargreaves, A, Hopkins, D and Lieberman, A (eds) *International Handbook of Education Change* (2nd ed, pp 445–67). New York: Springer Press.

Connelly, R, Sullivan, A and Jerrim, J (2014) *Primary and Secondary Education and Poverty Review*. York: Joseph Rowntree Foundation.

Cooper, K and Stewart, K (2013) *Does Money Affect Children's Outcomes?: A Systematic Review*. York: Joseph Rowntree Foundation.

Crawford, C, Dearden, L, Micklewright, J and Vignoles, A (2016) *Family Background and University Success: Differences in Higher Education Access and Outcomes in England*. Oxford: Oxford University Press.

Cremin, T and Myhill, D (2011) *Writing Voices: Creating Communities of Writers*. New York: Routledge.

Cremin, T and Oliver, L (2017) Teachers as Writers: A Systematic Review. *Research Papers in Education*, 32(3): 269–95.

Crossley, S (2017) *In Their Place: The Imagined Geographies of Poverty*. London: Pluto Press.

Cummins, J (2000) *Language, Power and Pedagogy*. Clevedon: Multilingual Matters.

Cummings, C, Laing, K, Law, J, McLaughlin, J, Papps, Todd, L and Woolner, P (2012) *Can Changing Aspirations and Attitudes Impact on Educational Attainment? A Review of Interventions*. York: Joseph Rowntree Foundation.

Daniels, H, Cole, T, Sellman, E, Sutton, J and Visser, J with Bedward, J (2003) *Study of Young People Permanently Excluded From School*. Birmingham: University of Birmingham.

Department for Children, Schools and Families (2008) *The Bercow Report: A Review of Services for Children and Young People (0–19) with Speech, Language and Communication Needs*. London: DCSF.

Department for Education (2010) *The Importance of Teaching: The Schools White Paper 2010*. London: DfE.

Department for Education (2013a) *Teachers' Standards Guidance for School Leaders, School Staff and Governing Bodies*. London: DfE.

Department for Education (2013b) *The National Curriculum in England (Framework Document)*. London: DfE.

Department for Education (2015) *Special Educational Needs in England*. London: DfE.

Department for Education (2017) *Permanent and Fixed Period Exclusions in England: 2015–16*. London: DfE.

Department for Education and Science (DfES) (2003) *Aiming High: Raising the Achievement of Minority Ethnic Pupils*. London: DfES.

Derry, J (2013) *Vygotsky Philosophy and Education*. London: Wiley Blackwell.

Dewey, J (1929) *The Sources of a Science of Education*. New York: Liveright.

Dickerson, A and Popli, G (2012) *Persistent Poverty and Children's Cognitive Development*. Evidence from the UK Millennium Cohort Study. London: Centre for Longitudinal Studies.

Dockrell, JE and Howell, P (2015) Identifying the Challenges and Opportunities to Meet the Needs of Children with Speech, Language and Communication Difficulties. *British Journal of Special Education*, 42(4): 411–28.

Dorling, D (2011) *Injustice: Why Social Inequality Persists*. Bristol: Policy Press.

Dorling, D (2015) *Injustice: Why Social Inequality Still Persists*. Bristol: Policy Press.

Duckworth, K and Schoon, I (2012) Beating the Odds: Exploring the Impact of Social Risk on Young People's School-to-work Transitions during Recession in the UK. *National Institute Economic Review*, 222(1): 38–51.

Dudley-Marling, C and Lucas, K (2009) Pathologizing the Language and Culture of Poor Children. *Language Arts*, 86(5): 362–70.

Egan, D (2017) *After PISA: A Way Forward for Education in Wales?* Merthyr Tydfil: Bevan Foundation.

Elliott, V, Baird, J, Hopfenbeck, T, Ingram, J, Thompson, I, Usher, N, Zantout, M, Richardson, J and Coleman, R (2016) *Approaches to Written Marking in English Primary and Secondary Schools: A Review*. London: Education Endowment Fund.

Elliott, V and Dingwall, N (2017) Roles as a Route to Being 'Other': Drama-based Interventions with At-risk Students. *Emotional and Behavioural Difficulties*, 22(1): 66–78.

Ellis, S, Thompson, I, McNicholl, J and Thomson, J (2016) Student Teachers' Perceptions of the Effects of Poverty on Learners' Educational Attainment and Well-being: Perspectives from England and Scotland. *Journal of Education for Teaching*, 42(4): 483–99.

Evans, GW (2004) The Environment of Childhood Poverty. *American Psychologist*, 59(2): 77–92.

Fancourt, N, Edwards, A and Menter, I (2015) Reimagining a School – University Partnership: The Development of the Oxford Education Deanery Narrative. *Education Inquiry*, 6(3): 353–73.

Fazel, M, Garica, J and Stein, A (2016) The Right Location? Experiences of Refugee Adolescents Seen by School-based Mental Health Services. *Clinical Child Psychology and Psychiatry*, 21: 368–80.

Fisher, R (2011) Failing to Learn or Learning to Fail? The Case of Young Writers, in Daniels, H and Hedegaard, M (eds) *Vygotsky and Special Needs Education* (pp 48–64) London: Continuum.

Fell, B and Hewstone, M (2015) *Psychological Perspectives on Poverty – Summary*. York: Joseph Rowntree Foundation.

Fleer, M and Hammer, M (2013) Emotions in Imaginative Situations: The Valued Place of Fairytales for Supporting Emotion Regulation. *Mind, Culture, and Activity*, 20(3): 240–59.

Fraser, N (1997) *Justice Interruptus*. London: Routledge.

Furlong, J and Lunt, I (2014) Inequality and Education: Continuing the Debate. *Oxford Review of Education*, 40(6): 667–79.

Gillborn, D (2008) *Racism and Education: Coincidence or Conspiracy?* London: Routledge.

Goddard, YL, Goddard, RD and Tschannen-Moran, M (2007) Theoretical and Empirical Investigation of Teacher Collaboration for School Improvement and Student Achievement in Public Elementary Schools. *Teachers College Record*, 109(4): 877–96.

González, N, Moll, LC and Amanti, C (2005) *Funds of Knowledge: Theorizing Practices in Households and Classrooms*. Mahwah, NJ: Erlbaum.

Gorard, S (2014) The Link between Academies in England, Pupil Outcomes and Local Patterns of Socioeconomic Segregation between Schools. *Research Papers in Education*, 29(3): 268–84.

Gorski, PC (2012) Perceiving the Problem of Poverty and Schooling: Deconstructing the Class Stereotypes that Mis-shape Education Practice and Policy. *Equity & Excellence in Education*, 45(2): 302–19.

Grudnoff, L, Haigh, M, Hill, M, Cochran-Smith, M, Ell, F and Ludlow, L (2016) Rethinking Initial Teacher Education: Preparing Teachers for Schools in Low Socio-economic Communities in New Zealand. *Journal of Education for Teaching*, 42(4): 451–67.

Haberman, M (1991) The Pedagogy of Poverty Versus Good Teaching. *Phi Delta Kappan*, 73(4): 290–4.

Hagger, H and McIntyre, D (2006) *Learning Teaching from Teachers: Realizing the Potential of School Based Teacher Education*. Maidenhead, UK: Open University Press.

Hammersley, M (2002) *Educational Research, Policymaking and Practice*. London: SAGE.

Hanley, L (2016) *Respectable: The Experience of Class*. London: Allen Lane.

Hattie, J (2003) Teachers Make a Difference: What Is the Research Evidence? Paper presented at the Building Teacher Quality: What Does the Research Tell Us ACER Research Conference, Melbourne, Australia.

Hayden, C (1996) Primary School Exclusions: The Need for Integrated Solutions, in Blyth, E and Milner, J (eds) *Exclusions from School: Inter-professional Issues in Policy and Practice* (pp 224–36). London: Routledge.

Hewitt-Main, J (2012) *Dyslexia Behind Bars*. Benfleet: Mentoring 4 U.

Hills, J, Brewer, M, Jenkins, SP, Lister, R, Lupton, R, Machin, S, Mills, C, Modood, T, Rees, T and Riddell, S (2010) *An Anatomy of Economic Inequality in the UK: Report of the National Equality Panel*. London: Centre for Analysis of Social Exclusion, London School of Economics and Political Science.

Horgan, G (2007) *The Impact of Poverty on Young Children's Experience of School*. York: Joseph Rowntree Foundation.

Hughes, J and Wilson, K (2004) Playing a Part: The Impact of Youth Theatre on Young People's Personal and Social Development. *Research in Drama Education: The Journal of Applied Theatre and Performance*, 9(1): 57–72.

Ivinson, G, Beckett, L, Egan, D, Leitch, R, McKinney, S, Thompson, I and Wrigley, T (2017) *BERA Commission on Poverty and Policy Advocacy Final Report*. London: BERA.

Jensen, E (2009) *Teaching with Poverty in Mind*. Alexandria, VA: ASCD.

Jones, O (2011) *Chavs: The Demonization of the Working Class*. London: Verso.

Kiernan, KE and Mensah, FK (2011) Poverty, Family Resources and Children's Early Educational Attainment: The Mediating Role of Parenting. *British Educational Research Journal*, 37(2): 317–36.

Ladson-Billings, G (2006) It's Not the Culture of Poverty, It's the Poverty of Culture: The Problem with Teacher Education. *Anthropology and Education Quarterly*, 37(2): 104–9.

Law, J and Sivyer, S (2003) Promoting the Communication Skills of Primary School Children Excluded from School or At Risk of Exclusion: An Intervention Study. *Child Language Teaching and Therapy*, 19(1): 1–25.

Lewin, K (1948) *Resolving Social Conflicts: Selected Papers on Group Dynamics*. New York: Harper and Row.

Lister, R (2004) *Poverty*. Cambridge: Polity Press.

Lumby, J (2013) Education Isn't Working for Us – Listening to Disengaged Young People. *BERA Insights*, (5): 1–4.

Lupton, R (2006) How Does Place Affect Education?, in Delorenzi, S (ed) *Going Places: Neighbourhood, Ethnicity and Social Mobility* (pp 59–71). London: Institute of Public Policy Research.

Lupton, R and Thrupp, M (2013) Headteachers' Readings of and Responses to Disadvantaged Contexts: Evidence from English Primary Schools. *British Educational Research Journal*, 39(4): 769–88.

Machin, S (2006) *Social Disadvantage and Education Experience*. Paris: OECD.

Mazzoli Smith, L and Todd, L (2016) *Poverty Proofing the School Day*. Newcastle: Newcastle University.

Machin, S and Silva, O (2013) School Structure, School Autonomy and the Tail. Centre for Economic Performance Special Paper No. 29. London: London School of Economics.

Macrae, S, Maguire, M and Milbourne, L (2003) Social Exclusion: Exclusion from School. *International Journal of Inclusive Education*, 7(2): 89–101.

McCoy, E (2013) *Lost for Words: Poor Literacy, the Hidden Issue in Child Poverty*. London: National Literacy Trust.

McCormick, J (2013) *A Review of Devolved Approaches to Child Poverty*. York: Joseph Rowntree Foundation.

McKinsey, J (2007) *How the World's Best-performing School Systems Come Out on Top*. London: McKinsey & Co.

McLeod, JD and Shanahan, MJ (1993) Poverty, Parenting and Children's Mental Health. *American Sociological Association*, 58(3): 351–66.

Menter, I and Thompson, I (2017) Closing the Evidence Gap? The Challenges of the Design, in Childs, A and Menter, I (eds) *Mobilising Teacher Researchers in England – A National Experiment*. London: Routledge.

Mercer, N (2000) *Words and Minds: How We Use Language to Think Together*. London: Routledge.

Miles, SB and Stipek, D (2006) Contemporaneous and Longitudinal Associations between Social Behavior and Literacy Achievement in a Sample of Low-income Elementary School Children. *Child Development*, 77: 103–17.

Milton Keynes Ethnic Minorities Support Service (2005) Supporting Learners with English as an Additional Language. Milton Keynes: Milton Keynes Council.

Murphy, VA, Kyriacou, M and Menon, P (2015) *Profiling Writing Challenges in Children with English as an Additional Language (EAL)*. Oxford: University of Oxford.

NATE (2016) *The National Curriculum for English from 2015*. London: NATE.

National Union of Teachers (2017) *Teacher Recruitment and Retention*. Retrieved from: www.teachers.org. uk/edufacts/teacher-recruitment-and-retention (accessed 15/09/17).

Newman, R, Talbot, J, Catchpole, R and Russell, L (2012) *Turning Young Lives around: How Health and Justice Services Can Respond to Children with Mental Health Problems and Learning Disabilities who Offend*. London: Prison Reform Trust.

OECD (Office of Economic Cooperation and Development) (2016) Who Are the Low-performing Students? *PISA in Focus, No. 60*. Paris: OECD Publishing.

Ofsted (2013) *Improving Literacy in Secondary Schools: Shared Responsibility*. Manchester: Ofsted.

Ortega, L, Thompson, I, Daniels, H and Tawell, A (2017) *Staff Collaboration in Secondary Schools: A Social Network Analysis of Advice-seeking Patterns Regarding Support for Vulnerable Students.* Paper presented at the ISCAR Congress, Quebec.

Osler, A, Watling, R and Busher, H (2001) *Reasons for Exclusion from School.* Research Report no. 244. London: DfEE.

Parkes, B (2012) Exclusion of Pupils from School in the UK. *The Equal Rights Review*, 8: 112–29.

Parsons, C (2005) School Exclusion: The Will to Punish. *British Journal of Educational Studies*, 53(2): 187–211.

Parsons, C and Platt L (2013) Disability Among Young Children: Prevalence, Heterogeneity and Socio-economic Disadvantage. CLS Working Paper 2013/11. London: Centre for Longitudinal Studies.

Parsons, S (2002) *Basic Skills and Crime: Findings from a Study of Adults Born in 1958 and 1970.* London: The Basic Skills Agency.

Pring, R (2013) *The Life and Death of Secondary Education for All.* London: Routledge.

Rack, J (2005) *The Incidence of Hidden Disabilities in the Prison Population.* Egham, Surrey: Dyslexia Institute.

Raffo, C, Dyson, A, Gunter, H, Hall, D, Jones, L and Kalambouka, A (2007) *Education and Poverty: A Critical Review of Theory, Policy and Practice.* York: Joseph Rowntree Foundation.

Rank, MR, Yoon, H-S and Hirschl, TA (2003) American Poverty as a Structural Failing: Evidence and Arguments. *Journal of Sociology and Social Welfare*, 30(4): 3–29.

Reynolds, D, Sullivan, M and Murgatroyd, S (1987) *The Comprehensive Experience.* Lewes: Falmer.

Ridge, T (2009) *Living with Poverty: A Review of the Literature on Children's and Families' Experiences of Poverty*, RR 594. London: Department for Work and Pensions.

Ripley, K and Yuill, N (2005) Patterns of Language Impairment and Behaviour in Boys Excluded from School. *British Journal of Educational Psychology*, 75: 37–50.

Robertson, D (2014) *Regeneration and Poverty in Scotland: Evidence and Policy Review.* Sheffield: Centre for Regional Economic and Social Research.

Russell, AE, Ford, T and Russell, G (2015) Socioeconomic Associations with ADHD: Findings from a Mediation Analysis. *PLoS ONE*, 10(6): e0128248. doi: 10.1371/journal.pone.0128248.

Sabel, C, Saxenian, A, Miettinen, R, Kristensen, PH and Hautamäki, J (2010) *Individualized Service Provision in the New Welfare State: Lessons from Special Education in Finland.* Helsinki: Report prepared for SITRA.

Sammons, P, Kington, A, Lindorff-Vijayendran, A and Ortega, L (2014) *Inspiring Teaching: What We Can Learn from Exemplary Practitioners.* Reading: CfBT.

Schwartz, E (1996) Why Many New Teachers are Unprepared to Teach in Most New York City Schools. *Phi Delta Kappan*, 78(1): 82–4.

Schweinhart, LJ (2003) *Benefits, Costs, and Explanation of the High/Scope Perry Preschool Program.* Paper presented at the Meeting of the Society for Research in Child Development. Tampa, Florida.

Shaw, B, Bernades, E, Trethewey, A and Menzies, L (2016) *Special Educational Needs and Their Links to Poverty.* York: Joseph Rowntree Foundation.

Shaw, B, Baars, S, Menzies, L, Parameshwaren, M and Allen, R (2017) *Low Income Pupils' Progress at Secondary School.* London: Social Mobility Commission.

Shildrick, T and Rucell, J (2015) *Sociological Perspectives on Poverty.* York: Joseph Rowntree Foundation.

Slee, R (2011) *The Irregular School: Exclusion, Schooling, and Inclusive Education.* London and New York: Routledge.

Smyth, J and Wrigley, T (2013) *Living on the Edge: Rethinking Poverty, Class and Schooling*. New York: Peter Lang.

Snowling, MJ, Adams, JW, Bowyer-Crane, C and Tobin, V (2000) Levels of Literacy Among Juvenile Offenders: The Incidence of Specific Reading Disabilities. *Criminal Behaviour and Mental Health*, 10(4): 229–41.

Sparkes, J and Glennerster, H (2002) Preventing Social Exclusion: Education's Contribution, in Hills, J, Le Grand, J and Pichaud, D (eds) *Understanding Social Exclusion*. Oxford: Oxford University Press.

Stamou, E, Edwards, A, Daniels, H and Ferguson, L (2014) *Young People At-risk of Drop-out from Education: Recognising and Responding to Their Needs*. Oxford: University of Oxford.

Strand, S (2014) Ethnicity, Gender, Social Class and Achievement Gaps at Age 16: Intersectionality and 'Getting it' for the White Working Class. *Research Papers in Education*, 29(2): 131–71.

Sullivan, A, Ketende, S and Joshi, H (2013) Social Class and Inequalities in Early Cognitive Scores. *Sociology*, 47(6): 1187–206.

Sutton Trust (2008) *Wasted Talent? Attrition Rates of High-achieving Pupils between School and University*. London: The Sutton Trust.

Sylva, K, Melhuish, E, Sammons, P, Siraj-Blatchford, I and Taggart, B (2004) *The Effective Provision of Pre-school Education (EPPE) Project: Findings from the Pre-school to the End of Key Stage* 1. London: DfES.

Tatto, M, Burn, K, Menter, I, Mutton, T and Thompson, I (2017) *Learning to Teach in England and the United States: The Evolution of Policy and Practice*. London: Routledge.

Thompson, I (2012a) Planes of Communicative Activity in Collaborative Writing. *Changing English*, 19(2): 209–20.

Thompson, I (2012b) Stimulating Reluctant Writers: A Vygotskian Approach to Teaching Writing in Secondary Schools. *English in Education*, 46(1): 84–91.

Thompson, I (2013) The Mediation of Learning in the Zone of Proximal Development through a Co-constructed Writing Activity. *Research in the Teaching of English*, 47(3): 247–76.

Thompson, I (2015) *Designing Tasks in Secondary Education: Enhancing Subject Understanding and Student Engagement*. London and New York: Routledge.

Thompson, I, McNicholl, J and Menter, I (2016) Student Teachers' Perceptions of Poverty and Educational Achievement. *Oxford Review of Education*, 42(2): 214–29.

Thompson, I and Tawell, A (2017) Becoming Other: Social and Emotional Development through the Creative Arts for Young People with Behavioural Difficulties. *Emotional and Behavioural Difficulties*, 22(1): 18–34.

Thompson, I and Wittek, L (2016) Writing as a Mediational Tool for Learning in the Collaborative Composition of Texts. *Learning, Culture and Social Interaction*, 11: 85–96.

Thorley, C (2016) *Education, Education, Mental Health: Supporting Secondary Schools to Play a Central Role in Early Intervention Mental Health Services*. London: Institute for Public Policy Research.

Thrupp, M, Mansell, H, Hawksworth, L and Harold, B (2003) 'Schools Can Make a Difference' – But Do Teachers, Heads and Governors Really Agree? *Oxford Review of Education*, 29(4): 471–84.

Vadeboncoeur, JA (2017) *Vygotsky and the Promise of Public Education*. New York: Peter Lang.

Visser, J (2005) Key Factors that Enable the Successful Management of Difficult Behaviour in Schools and Classrooms, *Education 3–13. International Journal of Primary, Elementary and Early Years Education*, 33(1): 26–31.

Vygotsky, LS (1987) Thinking and Speech, in Vygotsky, LS (ed) *Collected Works* (Vol 1, pp 39–285). New York: Plenum Press.

Vygotsky, LS (1993) *The Collected Works of L. S. Vygotsky. Vol. 2: The Fundamentals of Defectology.* New York: Plenum.

Wedge, P and Prosser, H (1973) *Born to Fail?* London: National Children's Bureau.

Wiliams, D (2015) The Research Delusion. Times Educational Supplement, April 10, 2015.

Wilkinson, R and Pickett, K (2010) *The Spirit Level – Why Equality is Better for Everyone.* London: Penguin.

Zeichner, K (2009) *Teacher Education and the Struggle for Social Justice.* New York and London: Routledge.

Zymont, E and Clark, P (2015) *Transforming Teacher Education for Social Justice.* New York: Teachers College Press.

INDEX

A

absolute poverty, 7
academisation process, 9
action research, 58–9
ADHD, *see* attention deficit hyperactivity disorder
adult/youth offending, 42–3
All-Party Parliamentary Group for Education, 49
Amanti, C, 47
attention deficit hyperactivity disorder
(ADHD), 16

B

Ball, S J, 31
Basic Interpersonal Communicative Skills
(BICS), 48
Basic Skills Agency, 43
BERA Commission on Poverty and Policy
Advocacy, 10
BICS, *see* Basic Interpersonal
Communicative Skills
Bramley, G, 31
British Council, 46
Brookes, M, 44
Bruner, J, 21
Bryan, K, 43
Buras, K L, 34

C

CALP, *see* Cognitive Academic Language
Proficiency
CAMHS, *see* child and adolescent mental health
services
Carlile, A, 44
child and adolescent mental health services
(CAMHS), 4
child poverty, 5–7
Child Poverty Act, 7
Child Poverty Action Group (CPAG), 6, 16
Child Poverty Strategy, 7
Children's Commission on Poverty, 32, 33
Clark, C, 41
classroom
assessing pupils' progress, 23–4
designing environment, 21–2
intervening outside, 61–2
pupil grouping and resourcing, 23
social learning, 20–1
Claxton, G, 22
Clegg, J, 44
Cognitive Academic Language Proficiency
(CALP), 48

cognitive effects, social and economic
disadvantage, 16
'contextual added value', 11
continuous professional development (CPD)
challenges, 13
Cooper, K, 6
costs of exclusion *versus* early prevention, 44–6
CPAG, *see* Child Poverty Action Group
Crawford, C, 31
Cremin, T, 44
culture of poverty, 34
Cummins, J, 33

D

deficit ideology, 34
deficit views of poverty
overview of, 33–4
Oxford case study, 36–7
social justice and ITE, 35
Strathclyde Literacy Clinic study, 37
through research, 35–6
Department for Education (DfE), 30
Department for Work and Pensions, 30
Derry, J, 22
Dewey, J, 58
Dickerson, A, 16
distributive theories, 2
Dorling, D, 6
Dudley-Marling, C, 34
Dugdale, G, 41

E

EAL, *see* English as an additional language
education
intervening outside classroom, 61–2
pupil premium grant (PPG), 59–61
Education Act 1944, 7
Education Endowment Foundation (EEF), 56
Education Policy Institute, 53
Education Reform Act 1988, 7
Education, Heath and Care (EHC) plan, 42
educational research *versus* educational
policy, 53–5
EEF, *see* Education Endowment Foundation
Egan, D, 13
Elliott, V, 23
emotion, role of, 24–5
England
policy difference, 11–12
Pupil Premium Grant, 11
English as an additional language (EAL), 46–9
environmental aspects of poverty, 17–18
Every Child Matters (ECM) agenda, 8

F

false dichotomy, 57
Fell, B, 16
fixed-term school exclusions, 41–2
Fraser, N, 3
free school meals (FSM), 30
free schooling, 32
Freer, J, 43
FSM, *see* free school meals
Furlong, C, 43

G

Goldacre, Ben, 55
González, N, 47
good teachers, features of, 21
Goodall, E, 44
Gorski, P C, 34
Gove, Michael, 9, 55

H

Hammersley, M, 54
Hattie, John, 57
Heady, L, 44
Hewitt-Main, J, 43
Hewstone, M, 16
Horgan, G, 28
Households Below Average Income
    statistics, 32

I

imagination, role of, 24–5
initial teacher education (ITE)
    challenges, 13
    clinical practice model, 57
Institute of Fiscal Studies, 6
intervening outside classroom, 61–2
ITE, *see* initial teacher education

J

Jensen, E, 32
Joseph Rowntree Foundation, 20
justice, theoretical conceptions of, 2

K

Kiernan, K E, 41

L

Labour Government Act 1976, 7
LAC, *see* language across the curriculum
Language for Life, 49

language impairment, 43–4
language, literacy and social disadvantages
    adult/youth offending, 42–3
    costs of exclusion *versus* early prevention,
        44–6
    difficulties, 40–1
    English as an additional language, 46–9
    fixed-term school exclusions, 41–2
    language impairment, 43–4
    literacy across the curriculum, 49–51
    literacy intervention *versus* costs of
        exclusion, 44–6
    permanent term school exclusions, 41–2
    reading impairment, 43–4
    school exclusions, 41
    Teachers as Writers, 51
    writing impairment, 43–4
Law, J, 42
Lewin, Kurt, 58
Lister, R, 3, 33
literacy across the curriculum (LAC), 49–51
literacy intervention *versus* costs of exclusion, 44–6
low-income pupils, 23
Lucas, K, 34

M

Macrae, S, 41
McCoy, E, 41
McGuire, M, 41
McNicholl, J, 3, 34
Mensah, F K, 41
mental health, 4
Menter, I, 3, 34
Mercer, N, 21
Milbourne, L, 41
Miles, S B, 45
Millennium Cohort Study (MCS), 16
Moll, L C, 47
MSC, *see* Millennium Cohort Study
Myhill, D, 44

N

NATE, *see* National Association of Teachers of
    English
National Association of Teachers of English
    (NATE), 50
National College for Teaching and Leadership
    (NCTL), 55
National Health Service (NHS), 4
National Literacy Trust, 41
National Union of Teachers (NUT), 4
NCTL, *see* National College for Teaching and
    Leadership
Newman, R, 43
NHS, *see* National Health Service
Northern Ireland, policy difference, 12
NUT, *see* National Union of Teachers

O

Oxford case study, deficit views of poverty, 36–7
Oxford Internship scheme, 57
Oxfordshire Local Education Authority, 57

P

Parsons, S, 45
pedagogy of poverty
    overview of, 28
    teachers influence, 28–9
    testing and performativity consequences, 29–30
permanent term school exclusions, 41–2
Perry Pre-school Programme, 45
persistent poverty, 7
Pickett, K, 6
policy difference
    England, 11–12
    Northern Ireland, 12
    Scotland, 12–13
    Wales, 13
policy history of disadvantage, 7–9
Popli, G, 16
poverty
    child, 5–7
    educational attainment and well-being, 30–2
    environmental aspects of, 17–18
    psychological effects of, 16–17
    real examples of children in, 32–3
    rural child, 31
    school day proofing, 33
    sociology of, 18–19
    special educational needs and disability, 19–20
PPG, see Pupil Premium Grant
practitioner research, 58–9
psychological effects, poverty, 16–17
pupil premium grant (PPG), 59–61

Q

qualified teacher shortage crisis, 4–5

R

Raffo, C, 56
Randomised Controlled Trails (RCTs), 55
RCTs, See Randomised Controlled Trails
reading impairment, 43–4
recognition theories, 2
reflexive research, 58
relative poverty, 7
research partnerships, 57
research, social disadvantage through, 25
Ridge, T, 29, 32
rural child poverty, 31

S

school exclusions, 41
schooling
    child poverty and, 5–7
    policy history of disadvantage, 7–9
schools
    continuous professional development (CPD) challenges, 13
    initial teacher education (ITE) challenges, 13
Scotland, policy difference, 12–13
SEND, see special educational needs and disability
Sivyer, S, 42
SNA, see Social Network Analysis
social disadvantage through research, 25
social inclusion, 9–10
social justice, 9–10
    deficit views of poverty, 35
    in education, 2–3
social learning, classroom, 20–1
social mobility, 9–10
Social Mobility and Child Poverty Commission 2012, 7
Social Mobility Commission, 25
Social Network Analysis (SNA), 25
sociology of poverty, 18–19
special educational needs and disability (SEND), 19–20
    definition of, 19
Stewart, K, 6
Stipek, D, 45
Strathclyde Literacy Clinic study, 37
Sutton Trust, 31
Sylva, K, 11

T

TAW, see Teachers as Writers
Tawell, A, 24
teacher collaboration, vulnerable learners, 25–7
teacher quality, 4
teachers as researchers, 56–7
Teachers as Writers (TAW), 51
teachers' standards, 4
TES, see Times Educational Supplement
testing and performativity consequences, 29–30
theoretical conceptions of justice, 2
Thompson, I, 3, 24, 34
Times Educational Supplement (TES), 57

U

UK Child Poverty Act 2010, 6
University of Oxford, 57

V

Vadeboncoeur, J A, 23
Visser, J, 45
vulnerable learners, teacher collaboration, 25–7
Vygotsky, L S, 21, 24

W

Wales, policy difference, 13
Welfare Reform and Work Act 2016, 7

Wilkinson, R, 6
Wilshaw, M, 49
writing impairment, 43–4

Z

Zeichner, K, 2, 3
zone of proximal development (ZPD), 21
ZPD, *see* zone of proximal development